Theory Of Conjugate Functions, Or Algebraic Couples

William Rowan Hamilton (sir.)

Professor Rigaud
with kind regards
from the author.

THEORY

OF

CONJUGATE FUNCTIONS,

OR

ALGEBRAIC COUPLES;

WITH A PRELIMINARY AND ELEMENTARY ESSAY ON

ALGEBRA AS THE SCIENCE OF PURE TIME.

BY WILLIAM ROWAN HAMILTON,

M. R. I. A., F. R. A. S., HON. M. R. S. ED. AND DUB., FELLOW OF THE AMERICAN ACADEMY OF ARTS AND SCIENCES AND OF THE ROYAL NORTHERN ANTIQUARIAN SOCIETY AT COPENHAGEN, ANDREWS' PROFESSOR OF ASTRONOMY IN THE UNIVERSITY OF DUBLIN, AND ROYAL ASTRONOMER OF IRELAND.

DUBLIN:
PRINTED BY PHILIP DIXON HARDY, 3, CECILIA-STREET.

1835.

Theory of Conjugate Functions, or Algebraic Couples; with a Preliminary and Elementary Essay on Algebra as the Science of Pure Time.

By WILLIAM ROWAN HAMILTON,

M.R.I.A., F.R.A.S., Hon. M.R.S. Ed. and Dub., Fellow of the American Academy of Arts and Sciences, and of the Royal Northern Antiquarian Society at Copenhagen, Andrews' Professor of Astronomy in the University of Dublin, and Royal Astronomer of Ireland.

Read November 4th, 1833, and June 1st, 1835.

General Introductory Remarks.

The Study of Algebra may be pursued in three very different schools, the Practical, the Philological, or the Theoretical, according as Algebra itself is accounted an Instrument, or a Language, or a Contemplation; according as ease of operation, or symmetry of expression, or clearness of thought, (the *agere*, the *fari*, or the *sapere*,) is eminently prized and sought for. The Practical person seeks a Rule which he may apply, the Philological person seeks a Formula which he may write, the Theoretical person seeks a Theorem on which he may meditate. The felt imperfections of Algebra are of three answering kinds. The Practical Algebraist complains of imperfection when he finds his Instrument limited in power; when a rule, which he could happily apply to many cases, can be hardly or not at all applied by him to some new case; when it fails to enable him to do or to discover something else, in some other Art, or in some other Science, to which Algebra with him was but subordinate, and for the sake of which and not for its own sake, he studied Algebra. The Philological Algebraist complains of imperfection, when his Language presents him with an Anomaly; when he finds an Exception disturb the simplicity of his Notation, or the symmetrical structure of his Syntax; when a Formula must be written with precaution, and a Symbolism is not universal. The Theoretical Algebraist complains of imperfection, when the clearness of his Contemplation is obscured; when the Reasonings of his Science seem anywhere to oppose each other, or become in any part too complex or too little valid for his belief to rest firmly upon them; or when, though trial may have taught him that a rule is useful, or that a formula gives true results, he cannot prove that rule, nor understand that formula: when he cannot rise to intuition from induction, or cannot look beyond the signs to the things signified.

It is not here asserted that every or any Algebraist belongs *exclusively* to any *one* of these three schools, so as to be *only* Practical, or *only* Philological, or *only* Theoretical. Language and Thought react, and Theory and Practice help each other. No man can be so merely practical as to use frequently the rules of Algebra, and never to admire the beauty of the language which expresses those rules, nor care to know the reasoning which deduces them. No man can be so merely philological an Algebraist but that things or thoughts will at some times intrude upon signs; and occupied as he may habitually be with the logical building up of his expressions, he will feel sometimes a desire to know what they mean, or to apply them. And no man can be so merely theoretical or so exclusively devoted to thoughts, and to the contemplation of theorems in Algebra, as not to feel an interest in its notation and language, its symmetrical system of signs, and the logical forms of their combinations; or not to prize those practical aids, and especially those methods of research, which the discoveries and contemplations of Algebra have given to other sciences. But, distinguishing without dividing, it is perhaps correct to say that every Algebraical Student and every Algebraical Composition may be referred upon the whole to one or other of these three schools, according as one or other of these three views habitually actuates the man, and eminently marks the work.

These remarks have been premised, that the reader may more easily and distinctly perceive what the design of the following communication is, and what the Author hopes or at least desires to accomplish. That design is *Theoretical,* in the sense already explained, as distinguished from what is Practical on the one hand, and from what is Philological upon the other. The thing aimed at, is to improve the *Science,* not the Art nor the Language of Algebra. The imperfections sought to be removed, are confusions of thought, and obscurities or errors of reasoning; not difficulties of application of an instrument, nor failures of symmetry in expression. And that confusions of thought, and errors of reasoning, still darken the beginnings of Algebra, is the earnest and just complaint of sober and thoughtful men, who in a spirit of love and honour have studied Algebraic Science, admiring, extending, and applying what has been already brought to light, and feeling all the beauty and consistence of many a remote deduction, from principles which yet remain obscure, and doubtful.

For it has not fared with the principles of Algebra as with the principles of Geometry. No candid and intelligent person can doubt the truth of the chief properties of *Parallel Lines,* as set forth by EUCLID in his Elements, two thousand years ago; though he may well desire to see them treated in a clearer and better method. The doctrine involves no obscurity nor confusion of thought, and leaves in the mind no reasonable ground for doubt, although ingenuity may usefully be exercised in improving the plan of the argument. But it requires no peculiar scepticism to doubt, or even to disbelieve, the doctrine of Negatives and Imaginaries, when set forth (as it has commonly been) with principles like these: that a *greater magnitude may be subtracted from a less,* and that the remainder is *less than nothing;* that *two negative numbers,* or numbers denoting magnitudes each less than nothing, may be *multiplied* the one by the other, and that the product will be a *positive* number, or a number denoting a magnitude greater than nothing; and that although the *square* of a number, or the product obtained by multiplying that number by itself, is therefore *always positive,* whether the number be positive or negative, yet that numbers, called *imaginary,* can be found or conceived or determined, and operated on by all the rules of positive and negative numbers, as if they were subject to those rules, *although they have negative squares,* and must therefore be supposed to be themselves neither positive nor negative, nor yet null numbers, so that the magnitudes which they are supposed to denote can neither be greater than nothing, nor less than nothing, nor even equal to nothing. It must be hard to found a SCIENCE on such grounds as these, though the forms of logic may build up from them a symmetrical system of expressions, and a practical art may be learned of rightly applying useful rules which seem to depend upon them.

So useful are those rules, so symmetrical those expressions, and yet so unsatisfactory those principles from which they are supposed to be derived, that a growing tendency may be perceived to the rejection of that view which regarded Algebra as a SCIENCE, *in some sense analogous to Geometry*, and to the adoption of one or other of those two different views, which regard Algebra as an *Art*, or as a *Language*: as a System of Rules, or else as a System of Expressions, but not as a System of *Truths*, or Results having any other validity than what they may derive from their practical usefulness, or their logical or philological coherence. Opinions thus are tending to substitute for the Theoretical question,—"Is a Theorem of Algebra *true*?" the Practical question,—"Can it be *applied as an Instrument*, to do or to discover something else, in some research which is not Algebraical?" or else the Philological question,—"Does its *expression harmonise*, according to the Laws of Language, with other Algebraical expressions?"

Yet a natural regret might be felt, if such were the destiny of Algebra; if a study, which is continually engaging mathematicians more and more, and has almost superseded the Study of Geometrical Science, were found at last to be not, in any strict and proper sense, the Study of a Science at all: and if, in thus exchanging the ancient for the modern Mathesis, there were a gain only of Skill or Elegance, at the expense of Contemplation and Intuition. Indulgence, therefore, may be hoped for, by any one who would inquire, whether existing Algebra, in the state to which it has been already unfolded by the masters of its rules and of its language, offers indeed no rudiment which may encourage a hope of developing a SCIENCE of Algebra: a Science properly so called; strict, pure, and independent; deduced by valid reasonings from its own intuitive principles; and thus not less an object of priori contemplation than Geometry, nor less distinct, in its own essence, from the Rules which it may teach or use, and from the Signs by which it may express its meaning.

The Author of this paper has been led to the belief, that the Intuition of TIME is such a rudiment.

This belief involves the three following as components: First, that the notion of Time is connected with existing Algebra; Second, that this notion or intuition of Time may be unfolded into an independent Pure Science; and Third, that the Science of Pure Time, thus unfolded, is co-extensive and identical with Algebra, so far as Algebra itself is a Science. The first component judgment is the result of an induction; the second of a deduction; the third is a joint result of the deductive and inductive processes.

I. The argument for the conclusion that *the notion of Time is connected with existing Algebra*, is an induction of the following kind. The History of Algebraic Science shows that the most remarkable discoveries in it have been made, either expressly through the medium of that notion of *Time*, or through the closely connected (and in some sort coincident) notion of *Continuous Progression*. It is the genius of Algebra to consider what it reasons on as *flowing*, as it was the genius of Geometry to consider what it reasoned on as *fixed*. EUCLID* defined a tangent to a circle, APOLLONIUS† conceived a tangent to an ellipse, as an indefinite straight line which had only one point in common with the curve; they looked upon the line and curve not as nascent or growing, but as already constructed and existing in space; they studied them as *formed* and *fixed*, they compared the one with the other, and the proved exclusion of any second common point was to them the essential property, the constitutive character of the tangent. The Newtonian Method of Tangents rests on another principle; it regards the curve and line not as

* Εὐθεῖα κύκλου ἐφάπτεσθαι λέγεται, ἥτις ἁπτομένη τοῦ κύκλου καὶ ἐκβαλλομένη οὐ τέμνει τὸν κύκλον.—EUCLID, Book III. Def. 2. Oxford Edition, 1703.

† Ἐὰν ἐν κώνου τομῇ ἀπὸ τῆς κορυφῆς τῆς τομῆς ἀχθῇ εὐθεῖα παρὰ τεταγμένως κατηγμένην, ἐκτὸς πεσεῖται τῆς τομῆς.—ἐκτὸς ἄρα πεσεῖται, διόπερ ἐφάπτεται τῆς τομῆς.—APPOLLONIUS, Book 1. Prop. 17. Oxford Edition, 1710.

already formed and fixed, but rather as ***nascent***, or in process of generation: and employs, as its primary conception, the thought of a ***flowing point***. And, generally, the revolution which NEWTON* made in the higher parts of both pure and applied Algebra, was founded mainly on the notion of ***fluxion***, which involves the notion of *Time*.

Before the age of NEWTON, another great revolution, in Algebra as well as in Arithmetic, had been made by the invention of ***Logarithms***; and the "Canon Mirificus" attests that NAPIER† deduced that invention, not (as it is commonly said) from the arithmetical properties of powers of numbers, but from the contemplation of a ***Continuous Progression***; in describing which, he speaks expressly of ***Fluxions***, ***Velocities*** and ***Times***.

In a more modern age, LAGRANGE, in the Philological spirit, sought to reduce the Theory of Fluxions to a system of operations upon symbols, analogous to the earliest symbolic operations of Algebra, and professed to reject the notion of time as foreign to such a system; yet admitted‡ that fluxions might be considered only as the velocities with which magnitudes vary, and that in so considering them, abstraction might be made of every mechanical idea. And in one of his own most important researches in pure Algebra, (the investigation of limits between which the sum of any number of terms in TAYLOR's Series is comprised,) LAGRANGE‖ employs the conception of ***continuous progression*** to show that a certain variable quantity may be made as small as can be desired. And not to dwell on the beautiful discoveries made by the same great mathematician, in the theory of singular primitives of equations, and in the algebraical dynamics of the heavens, through an extension of the conception of ***variability***, (that is, in fact, of ***flowingness***,) to quantities which had before been viewed as ***fixed*** or constant, it may suffice for the present to observe that LAGRANGE considered Algebra to be the ***Science of Functions***§, and that it is not easy to conceive a clearer or juster idea of a ***Function*** in this Science, than by regarding its essence as consisting in a ***Law connecting Change with Change***. But where ***Change*** and ***Progression*** are, there is TIME. The notion of Time is, therefore, inductively found to be connected with existing Algebra.¶

II. The argument for the conclusion that ***the notion of time may be unfolded into an independent Pure Science***, or that ***a Science of Pure Time is possible***, rests chiefly on the existence of certain priori

* Considerando igitur quod quantitates æqualibus temporibus crescentes et crescendo genitæ, pro velocitate majori vel minori qua crescunt ac generantur evadunt majores vel minores; methodum quærebam determinandi quantitates ex velocitatibus motuum vel incrementorum quibus generantur; et has motuum vel incrementorum velocitates nominando *Fluxiones*, et quantitates genitas nominando *Fluentes*, incidi paulatim annis 1665 et 1666 in Methodum Fluxionum qua hic usus sum in Quadratura Curvarum—*Tractatus de Quad. Curv.*, Introd., published at the end of Sir I. Newton's Opticks, London 1704.

† Logarithmus ergò cujusque sinus, est numerus quam proximè definiens lineam, quæ æqualiter crevit intereà dum sinus totius linea proportionaliter in sinum illum decrevit, existente utroque motu synchrono, atque initio æquiveloce. Baron Napier's *Mirifici Logarithmorum Canonis Descriptio*, Def. 6, Edinburgh 1614.—Also in the explanation of Def. 1, the words *fluxu* and *fluat* occur.

‡ Calcul des Fonctions, Leçon Premiere, page 2. Paris 1806.

‖ Donc puisque V devient nul lorsque i devient nul, il est clair qu' en faisant croître i par degrés insensibles depuis zéro, la valeur de V croîtra aussi insensiblement depuis zéro, soit en plus ou en moins, jusqu' à un certain point, après quoi elle pourra diminuer.—Calcul des Fonctions, Leçon Neuvième, page 90. Paris 1806. An instance still more strong may be found in the First Note to Lagrange's *Equations Numeriques*. Paris, 1808.

§ On doit regarder l'algèbre comme la science des fonctions.—Calc. des Fonct., Leçon Premiere.

¶ The word "Algebra" is used throughout this whole paper, in the sense which is commonly but improperly given by modern mathematical writers to the name "Analysis," and not with that narrow signification to which the unphilosophical use of the latter term (Analysis) has caused the former term (Algebra) to be too commonly confined. The author confesses that he has often deserved the censure which he has here so freely expressed.

intuitions, connected with that notion of time, and fitted to become the sources of a pure Science; and on the actual deduction of such a Science from those principles, which the author conceives that he has begun. Whether he has at all succeeded in *actually effecting* this deduction, will be judged after the Essay has been read; but that such a deduction is *possible*, may be concluded in an easier way, by an appeal to those intuitions to which allusion has been made. That a moment of time respecting which we inquire, as compared with a moment which we know, must either coincide with or precede or follow it, is an intuitive truth, as certain, as clear, and as unempirical as this, that no two straight lines can comprehend an area. The notion or intuition of ORDER IN TIME is not less but more deep-seated in the human mind, than the notion or intuition of ORDER IN SPACE; and a mathematical Science may be founded on the former, as pure and as demonstrative as the science founded on the latter. There is something mysterious and transcendent involved in the idea of Time; but there is also something definite and clear: and while Metaphysicians meditate on the one, Mathematicians may reason from the other.

III. That the *Mathematical Science of Time*, when sufficiently unfolded, and distinguished on the one hand from all actual Outward Chronology (or collections of recorded events and phenomenal marks and measures), and on the other hand from all Dynamical Science (or reasonings and results from the notion of cause and effect), will ultimately be found to be co-extensive and identical with Algebra, so far as Algebra itself is a Science: is a conclusion to which the author has been led by all his attempts, whether to *analyse* what is *Scientific in Algebra*, or to *construct* a *Science of Pure Time*. It is a joint result of the inductive and deductive processes, and the grounds on which it rests could not be stated in a few general remarks. The author hopes to explain them more fully in a future paper; meanwhile he refers to the present one, as removing (in his opinion) the difficulties of the usual theory of Negative and Imaginary Quantities, or rather substituting a new Theory of *Contrapositives* and *Couples*, which he considers free from those old difficulties, and which is deduced from the Intuition or Original Mental Form of Time: the opposition of the (so-called) Negatives and Positives being referred by him, *not* to the opposition of the operations of increasing and diminishing a *magnitude*, but to the simpler and more extensive contrast between the relations of *Before* and *After*,* or between the directions of *Forward* and *Backward*; and *Pairs of Moments* being used to suggest a *Theory of Conjugate Functions*,† which gives reality and meaning to conceptions that were before Imaginary,‡ Impossible, or Contradictory, because Mathematicians had derived them from that bounded notion of *Magnitude*, instead of the original and comprehensive thought of ORDER IN PROGRESSION.

* It is, indeed, very common, in Elementary works upon Algebra, to allude to *past and future time*, as one among many *illustrations* of the doctrine of negative quantities; but this avails little for Science, so long as *magnitude* instead of PROGRESSION is attempted to be made the *basis* of the doctrine.

† The author was conducted to this Theory many years ago, in reflecting on the important symbolic results of Mr. GRAVES respecting Imaginary Logarithms, and in attempting to explain to himself the theoretical meaning of those remarkable symbolisms. The Preliminary and Elementary Essay on Algebra as the Science of Pure Time, is a much more recent developement of an Idea against which the author struggled long, and which he still longer forbore to make public, on account of its departing so far from views now commonly received. The novelty, however, is in the view and method, not in the results and details: in which the reader is warned to expect little addition, if any, to what is already known.

‡ The author acknowledges with pleasure that he agrees with M. CAUCHY, in considering every (so-called) Imaginary Equation as a symbolic representation of two separate Real Equations: but he differs from that excellent mathematician in his method generally, and especially in not introducing the sign $\sqrt{-1}$ until he has provided for it, by his Theory of Couples, a possible and real meaning, as a symbol of the couple (0,1).

CONTENTS OF THE PRELIMINARY AND ELEMENTARY ESSAY ON ALGEBRA AS THE SCIENCE OF PURE TIME.

CONTENTS OF THE THEORY OF CONJUGATE FUNCTIONS, OR ALGEBRAIC COUPLES.

PRELIMINARY AND ELEMENTARY ESSAY

ON ALGEBRA AS THE SCIENCE OF PURE TIME.

Comparison of any two moments with respect to identity or diversity, subsequence or precedence.

1. If we have formed the *thought* of any one moment of time, we may afterwards either *repeat* that thought, or else think of a *different* moment. And if any two spoken or written *names*, such as the letters A and B, be *dates*, or answers to the question *When*, denoting each a known moment of time, they must either be names of one and the *same* known moment, or else of two *different* moments. In each case, we may speak of the *pair of dates* as denoting a *pair of moments*; but in the first case, the two moments are coincident, while in the second case they are distinct from each other. To express concisely the former case of relation, that is, the case of *identity* between the moment named B and the moment named A, or of *equivalence* between the date B and the date A, it is usual to write

$$B = A; \qquad (1.)$$

a written sentence or assertion, which is commonly called an *equation*: and to express concisely the latter case of relation, that is, the case of *diversity* between the two moments, or of *non-equivalence* between the two dates, we may write

$$B \neq A; \qquad (2.)$$

3. When the foregoing relation between four moments A B C D does not exist, that is, when the pairs AB and CD are not analogous pairs, we may mark this *non-analogy* by writing

$$D - C \mp B - A; \qquad (15.)$$

and the two possible cases into which this general conception of non-analogy or diversity of relation subdivides itself, namely, the case when the analogy fails on account of the moment D being *too late*, and the case when it fails because that moment D is *too early*, may be denoted, respectively, by writing in the first case,

$$D - C > B - A, \qquad (16.)$$

and in the second case,

$$D - C < B - A; \qquad (17.)$$

while the two cases themselves may be called, respectively, a *non-analogy of subsequence*, and a *non-analogy of precedence*. We may also say that the relation of D to C, as compared with that of B to A, is in the first case a relation of *comparative lateness*, and in the second case a relation of *comparative earliness*.

Alternations and inversions may be applied to these expressions of non-analogy, and the case of D *too late* may be expressed in any one of the eight following ways, which are all equivalent to each other,

$$\left.\begin{array}{ll} D - C > B - A, & B - A < D - C, \\ D - B > C - A, & C - A < D - B, \\ C - D < A - B, & A - B > C - D, \\ B - D < A - C, & A - C > B - D; \end{array}\right\} \qquad (18.)$$

while the other case, when the analogy fails because the moment D is *too early*, may be expressed at pleasure in any of the eight ways following,

$$\left.\begin{array}{ll} D - C < B - A, & B - A > D - C, \\ D - B < C - A, & C - A > D - B, \\ C - D > A - B, & A - B < C - D, \\ B - D > A - C, & A - C < B - D. \end{array}\right\} \qquad (19.)$$

In general, if we have any analogy or non-analogy between two pairs of moments, A B and C D, of which we may call the first and fourth mentioned moments, A and D, the *extremes*, and the second and third mentioned moments, namely, B and C, the *means*, and may call A and C the *antecedents*, and B and D the *consequents*; we do not disturb this analogy or non-analogy by interchanging the means among themselves, or the extremes among themselves; or by altering equally, in direction and in degree, the two consequents, or the two antecedents, of the analogy or of the non-analogy, or the two moments of either pair; or, finally, by altering oppositely in direction, and equally in degree, the two extremes, or the two means. In an analogy, we may also put, by inversion, extremes for means, and means for extremes; but if a non-analogy be thus inverted, it must afterwards be changed in kind, from subsequence to precedence, or from precedence to subsequence.

Combinations of two different analogies, or non-analogies, of pairs of moments, with each other.

4. From the remarks last made, it is manifest that

$$\left.\begin{array}{l} \text{if } \quad D - C = B - A, \\ \text{and } D' - D = B' - B, \\ \text{then } D' - C = B' - A; \end{array}\right\} \qquad (20.)$$

because the second of these three analogies shews, that in passing from the first to the third, we have either made no change, or only altered equally in direction and in degree the two consequent moments B and D of the first analogy. In like manner,

$$\left.\begin{array}{l} \text{if } \quad D - C = B - A, \\ \text{and } C' - C = A' - A, \\ \text{then } D - C' = B - A'; \end{array}\right\} \qquad (21.)$$

because now, in passing from the first to the third analogy, the second analogy shews that we have either made no change, or else have only altered equally, in direction and degree, the antecedents A and C. Again,

$$\left.\begin{array}{l} \text{if } \quad D - C = B - A, \\ \text{and } D' - D = C' - C, \\ \text{then } D' - C' = B - A; \end{array}\right\} \qquad (22.)$$

because here we have only altered equally, if at all, the two moments C and D of one common pair, in passing from the first analogy to the third. Again,

$$\left.\begin{array}{l} \text{if } \quad D - C = B - A, \\ \text{and } C - C' = B' - B, \\ \text{then } D - C' = B' - A; \end{array}\right\} \qquad (23.)$$

because now we either do not alter the means B and C at all, or else alter them oppositely in direction and equally in degree. And similarly,

$$\left.\begin{array}{l}\text{if } \quad D - C = B - A,\\ \text{and } D' - D = A - A',\\ \text{then } D' - C = B - A',\end{array}\right\} \qquad (24.)$$

because here we only alter equally, if at all, in degree, and oppositely in direction, the extremes, A and D, of the first analogy. It is still more evident that if two pairs be analogous to the same third pair, they are analogous to each other; that is

$$\left.\begin{array}{l}\text{if } \quad D - C = B - A,\\ \text{and } B - A = D' - C',\\ \text{then } D - C = D' - C'.\end{array}\right\} \qquad (25.)$$

And each of the foregoing conclusions will still be true, if we change the first supposed analogy $D - C = B - A$, to a non-analogy of subsequence $D - C > B - A$, or to a non-analogy of precedence $D - C < B - A$, provided that we change, in like manner, the last or concluded analogy to a non-analogy of subsequence in the one case, or of precedence in the other.

It is easy also to see, that if we still suppose the first analogy $D - C = B - A$ to remain, we cannot conclude the third analogy, and are not even at liberty to suppose that it exists, in any one of the foregoing combinations, unless we suppose the second also to remain: that is, if two analogies have the same antecedents, they must have analogous consequents; if the consequents be the same in two analogies, the antecedents must themselves form two analogous pairs; if the extremes of one analogy be the same with the extremes of another, the means of either may be combined as extremes with the means of the other as means, to form a new analogy; if the means of one analogy be the same with the means of another, then the extremes of either may be combined as means with the extremes of the other as extremes, and the resulting analogy will be true; from which the principle of inversion enables us farther to infer, that if the extremes of one analogy be the same with the means of another, then the means of the former may be combined as means with the extremes of the latter as extremes, and will thus generate another true analogy.

On continued Analogies, or Equidistant Series of Moments.

5. It is clear from the foregoing remarks, that in any analogy

$$B' - A' = B - A, \qquad (26.)$$

the two moments of either pair A B or A' B' cannot coincide, and so reduce themselves to one single moment, without the two moments of the other pair A′ B′ or A B being also identical with each other; nor can the two antecedents A A′ coincide, without the two consequents B B′ coinciding also, nor can the consequents without the antecedents. The only way, therefore, in which two of the four moments A B A′ B′ of an analogy can coincide, without the two others coinciding also, that is, the only way in which an analogy can be constructed with three distinct moments of time, is either by the two extremes A B′ coinciding, or else by the two means B A′ coinciding; and the principle of inversion permits us to reduce the former of these two cases to the latter. We may then take as a sufficient type of every analogy which can be constructed with three distinct moments, the following:

$$\text{B}' - \text{B} = \text{B} - \text{A}; \qquad (27.)$$

that is, the case when an extreme moment B′ is related to a mean moment B, as that mean moment B is related to another extreme moment A; in which case we shall say that the three moments A B B′ compose a *continued analogy*. In such an analogy, it is manifest that the three moments A B B′ compose also an *equidistant series*, B′ being exactly so much later or so much earlier than B, as B is later or earlier than A. The moment B is evidently, in this case, exactly intermediate between the two other moments A and B′, and may be therefore called *the middle moment*, or the *bisector*, of the interval of time between them. It is clear that whatever two distinct moments A and B′ may be, there is always one and only one such bisector moment B; and that thus a continued analogy between three moments can always be constructed in one but in only one way, by inserting a mean, when the extremes are given. And it is still more evident, from what was shewn before, that the middle moment B, along with either of the extremes, determines the other extreme, so that it is always possible to complete the analogy in one but in only one way, when an extreme and the middle are given.

6. If, besides the continued analogy (27.) between the three moments A B B′, we have also a continued analogy between the two last B B′ of these three and a fourth moment B″, then the *four* moments A B B′ B″ may themselves also be said to form another *continued analogy*, and an *equidistant series*, and we may express their relations as follows:

$$\text{B}'' - \text{B}' = \text{B}' - \text{B} = \text{B} - \text{A}. \qquad (28.)$$

In this case, the interval between the two extreme moments A and B″ is *trisected* by the two intermediate moments B and B′, and we may call B the *first trisector*, and B′ the *second trisector* of that interval. If the first extreme moment A and the first trisector moment B be given, it is evidently possible to complete the continued analogy or equidistant series in one and in only one way, by supplying the second trisector B′ and the second extreme B″; and it is not much less easy to perceive that any two of the four moments being given, (together with their names of position in the series, as such particular extremes, or such particular trisectors,) the two other moments can be determined, as necessarily connected with the given ones. Thus, if the extremes be given, we must conceive their interval as capable of being trisected by two means, in one and in only one way; if the first extreme and second trisector be given, we can bisect the interval between them, and so determine (in thought) the first trisector, and afterwards the second extreme; if the two trisectors be given, we can continue their interval equally in opposite directions, and thus determine (in thought) the two extremes; and if either of these two trisectors along with the last extreme be given, we can determine, by processes of the same kind, the two other moments of the series.

7. In general, we can imagine a continued analogy and an equidistant series, comprising any number of moments, and having the interval between the extreme moments of the series divided into the next lesser number of portions equal to each other, by a number of intermediate moments which is itself the next less number to the number of those equal portions of the whole interval. For example, we may imagine an equidistant series of five moments, with the interval between the two extremes divided into four partial and mutually equal intervals, by three intermediate moments, which may be called the first, second, and third *quadrisectors* or quarterers of the total interval. And it is easy to perceive, that when any two moments of an equidistant series are given, (as such or such known moments of time,) together with their places in that series, (as such particular extremes, or such particular intermediate moments,) the other moments of the series can then be all determined; and farther, that the series itself may be continued forward and backward, so as to include an unlimited number of new moments, without losing its character of equidistance. Thus, if we know the first extreme moment A, and the third quadrisector B″ of the total interval (from A to B‴) in any equidistant series of five moments, A B B′ B″ B‴, we can determine by trisection the two first quadrisectors B and B′, and afterwards the last extreme moment B‴; and may then continue the series, forward and backward, so as to embrace other moments B^{iv}, B^{v}, &c., beyond the fifth of those originally conceived, and others also such as E, E′, E″, &c., behind the first of the original five moments, that is, preceding it in the order of progression of the series; these new moments forming with the old an equidistant series of moments, (which comprehends as a part of itself the original series of five,) namely, the following unlimited series,

$$\ldots \mathrm{E}'' \mathrm{E}' \mathrm{E} \mathrm{A} \mathrm{B} \mathrm{B}' \mathrm{B}'' \mathrm{B}''' \mathrm{B}^{\mathrm{IV}} \mathrm{B}^{\mathrm{V}} \ldots, \qquad (29.)$$

constructed so as to satisfy the conditions of a continued analogy,

$$\ldots \mathrm{B}^{\mathrm{V}} - \mathrm{B}^{\mathrm{IV}} = \mathrm{B}^{\mathrm{IV}} - \mathrm{B}''' = \mathrm{B}''' - \mathrm{B}'' = \mathrm{B}'' - \mathrm{B}' = \mathrm{B}' - \mathrm{B} = \mathrm{B} - \mathrm{A} = \mathrm{A} - \mathrm{E} = \mathrm{E} - \mathrm{E}' = \mathrm{E}' - \mathrm{E}'' \ldots \qquad (30.)$$

8. By thus constructing and continuing an equidistant series, of which any two moments are given, we can arrive at other moments, as far from those two, and as near to each other, as we desire. For no moment B can be so distant from a given moment A, (on either side of it, whether as later or as earlier,) that we cannot find others still more distant, (and on the same side of A, still later or still earlier,) by continuing (in both directions) any given analogy, or given equidistant series; and, therefore, no two given moments, C and D, if not entirely coincident, can possibly be so near to each other, that we cannot find two moments still more near by treating any two given distinct moments (A and B), whatever, as extremes of an equidistant series of moments sufficiently many, and by inserting the appropriate means, or intermediate moments, between those two given extremes. Since, however far it may be necessary to continue the equidistant series C D...D$^{\prime}$, with C and D for its two first moments, in order to arrive at a moment D$^{\prime}$ more distant from C than B is from A, it is only necessary to insert as many intermediate moments between A and B as between C and D$^{\prime}$, in order to generate a new equidistant series of moments, each nearer to the one next it than D to C. Three or more moments A B C &c. may be said to be *uniserial* with each other, when they all belong to one common continued analogy, or equidistant series; and though we have not proved (and shall find it not to be true) that *any* three moments whatever are thus uniserial moments, yet we see that if any two moments be given, such as A and B, we can always find a third moment B$^{\prime}$ uniserial with these two, and differing (in either given direction) by less than any interval proposed from any given third moment C, whatever that may be. This possibility of indefinitely appproaching (on either side) to any given moment C, by moments uniserial with any two given ones A and B, increases greatly the importance which would otherwise belong to the theory of continued analogies, or equidistant series of moments. Thus if any two given dates, C and D, denote two distinct moments of time, (C $\neq$ D,) however near to each other they may be, we can always conceive their diversity detected by inserting means sufficiently numerous between any two other given distinct moments A and B, as the extremes of an equidistant series, and then, if necessary, extending this series in both directions beyond those given extremes, until some one of the moments B$^{\prime}$ of the equidistant series thus generated is found to fall between the two near moments C and D, being later than the earlier, and earlier than

the later of those two. And, therefore, reciprocally, if in any case of two given dates C and D, we can prove that no moment B′ *whatever*, of all that can be imagined as uniserial with two given distinct moments A and B, falls thus between the moments C and D, we shall then have a sufficient proof that those two moments C and D are identical, or, in other words, that the two dates C and D represent only one common moment of time, (C=D,) and not two different moments, however little asunder.

And even in those cases in which we have not yet succeeded in discovering a rigorous proof of this sort, identifying a sought moment with a known one, or distinguishing the former from the latter, the conception of continued analogies offers always a method of research, and of nomenclature, for investigating and expressing, or, at least, conceiving as investigated and expressed, with any proposed degree of approximation if not with perfect accuracy, the situation of the sought moment in the general progression of time, by its relation to a known equidistant series of moments sufficiently close. This might, perhaps, be a proper place, in a complete treatise on the *Science of Pure Time*, to introduce a regular system of *integer ordinals*, such as the words *first, second, third,* &c., with the written marks 1, 2, 3, &c., which answer both to them and to the *cardinal* or quotitative numbers, *one, two, three,* &c.; but it is permitted and required, by the plan of the present essay, that we should treat these spoken and written names of the integer ordinals and cardinals, together with the elementary laws of their combinations, as already known and familiar. It is the more admissible in point of method to suppose this previous acquaintance with the chief properties of integer numbers, as set forth in elementary arithmetic, because these properties, although belonging to the Science of Pure Time, as involving the conception of succession, may all be deduced from the unfolding of that mere conception of *succession,* (among things or thoughts as *counted,*) without requiring any notion of *measurable intervals*, equal or unequal, between successive moments of time. Arithmetic, or the *science of counting*, is, therefore, a part, indeed, of the *Science of Pure Time*, but a part so simple and familiar that it may be presumed to have been previously and separately studied, to some extent, by any one who is entering on Algebra.

On steps in the progression of time; their application (direct or inverse) to moments, so as to generate other moments; and their combination with other steps, in the way of composition or decomposition.

9. The foregoing remarks may have sufficiently shewn the importance, in the general study of pure time, of the conception of a continued analogy or equidistant

series of moments. This conception involves and depends on the conception of the repeated transference of one common ordinal relation, or the continued application of one common mental step, by which we pass, in thought, from any moment of such a series to the moment immediately following. For this, and for other reasons, it is desirable to study, generally, the properties and laws of the transference, or application, direct or inverse, and of the composition or decomposition, of ordinal relations between moments, or of steps in the progression of time; and to form a convenient system of written signs, for concisely expressing and reasoning on such applications and such combinations of steps.

In the foregoing articles, we have denoted, by the complex symbol B − A, the ordinal relation of the moment B to the moment A, whether that relation were one of identity or of diversity; and if of diversity, then whether it were one of subsequence or of precedence, and in whatever degree. Thus, having previously interposed the mark = between two equivalent signs for one common moment of time, we came to interpose the same sign of equivalence between any two marks of one ordinal relation, and to write

$$D - C = B - A,$$

when we designed to express that the relations of D to C and of B to A were coincident, being both relations of identity, or both relations of diversity; and if the latter, then both relations of subsequence, or both relations of precedence, and both in the same degree. In like manner, having agreed to interpose the mark $\ddagger$ between the two signs of two moments essentially different from each other, we wrote

$$D - C \ddagger B - A,$$

when we wished to express that the ordinal relation of D to C (as identical, or subsequent, or precedent) did *not* coincide with the ordinal relation of the moment B to A; and, more particularly, when we desired to distinguish between the two principal cases of this non-coincidence of relations, namely the case when the relation of D to C (as compared with that of B to A) was comparatively a relation of lateness, and the case when the same relation (of D to C) was comparatively a relation of earliness, we wrote, in the first case,

$$D - C > B - A,$$

and in the second case,

$$D - C < B - A,$$

having previously agreed to write

$$B > A$$

if the moment B were later than the moment A, or

$$B < A$$

if B were earlier than A.

Now, without yet altering at all the foregoing conception of $B-A$, as the symbol of an *ordinal relation* discovered by the comparison of two moments, we may in some degree abridge and so far simplify all these foregoing expressions, by using a simpler symbol of relation, such as a single letter a or b &c. or in some cases the character 0, or other simple signs, instead of a complex symbol such as $B-A$, or $D-C$, &c. Thus, if we agree to use the symbol 0 to denote the relation of identity between two moments, writing

$$A-A=0, \qquad (31.)$$

we may express the equivalence of any two dates B and A, by writing

$$B-A=0, \qquad (32.)$$

and may express the non-equivalence of two dates by writing

$$B-A \neq 0; \qquad (33.)$$

distinguishing the two cases when the moment B is later and when it is earlier than A, by writing, in the first case,

$$B-A>0, \qquad (34.)$$

and in the second case,

$$B-A<0, \qquad (35.)$$

to express, that as compared with the relation of identity 0, the relation $B-A$ is in the one case a relation of comparative lateness, and in the other case a relation of comparative earliness: or, more concisely, by writing, in these four last cases respectively, which were the cases before marked (1.) (2.) (3.) and (4.),

$$a=0, \qquad (36.)$$

$$a \neq 0, \qquad (37.)$$

$$a>0, \qquad (38.)$$

$$a<0, \qquad (39.)$$

if we put, for abridgement,

$$B-A=a. \qquad (40.)$$

Again, if we put, in like manner, for abridgement,

$$D-C=b, \qquad (41.)$$

the analogy (10.) namely,

$$\text{D} - \text{C} = \text{B} - \text{A},$$

may be concisely expressed as follows,

$$\mathfrak{b} = \mathfrak{a}; \qquad (42.)$$

while the general non-analogy (15.),

$$\text{D} - \text{C} \mathrel{\mp} \text{B} - \text{A},$$

may be expressed thus,

$$\mathfrak{b} \mathrel{\mp} \mathfrak{a}, \qquad (43.)$$

and the written expressions of its two cases (16.) and (17.), namely,

$$\text{D} - \text{C} > \text{B} - \text{A}$$

$$\text{and} \quad \text{D} - \text{C} < \text{B} - \text{A},$$

may be abridged in the following manner,

$$\mathfrak{b} > \mathfrak{a}, \qquad (44.)$$

$$\text{and} \quad \mathfrak{b} < \mathfrak{a}. \qquad (45.)$$

Again, to denote a relation which shall be exactly the inverse or opposite of any proposed ordinal relation $\mathfrak{a}$ or $\mathfrak{b}$, we may agree to employ a complex symbol such as $\Theta\,\mathfrak{a}$ or $\Theta\,\mathfrak{b}$, formed by prefixing the mark Θ, (namely, the initial letter O of the Latin word Oppositio, distinguished by a bar across it, from the same letter used for other purposes,) to the mark $\mathfrak{a}$ or $\mathfrak{b}$ of the proposed ordinal relation; that is, we may agree to use $\Theta\,\mathfrak{a}$ to denote the ordinal relation of the moment A to B, or $\Theta\,\mathfrak{b}$ to denote the ordinal relation of C to D, when the symbol $\mathfrak{a}$ has been already chosen to denote the relation of B to A, or $\mathfrak{b}$ to denote that of D to C: considering the two assertions

$$\text{B} - \text{A} = \mathfrak{a}, \text{ and } \text{A} - \text{B} = \Theta\,\mathfrak{a}, \qquad (46.)$$

as equivalent each to the other, and in like manner the two assertions

$$\text{D} - \text{C} = \mathfrak{b}, \text{ and } \text{C} - \text{D} = \Theta\,\mathfrak{b}, \qquad (47.)$$

and similarly in other cases. In this notation, the theorems (5.) (6.) (7.) (8.) may be thus respectively written:

$$\Theta\,\mathfrak{a} = 0, \text{ if } \mathfrak{a} = 0; \qquad (48.)$$

$$\Theta\,\mathfrak{a} \mathrel{\mp} 0, \text{ if } \mathfrak{a} \mathrel{\mp} 0; \qquad (49.)$$

$$\Theta\,\mathfrak{a} < 0, \text{ if } \mathfrak{a} > 0; \qquad (50.)$$

$$\Theta\,\mathfrak{a} > 0, \text{ if } \mathfrak{a} < 0; \qquad (51.)$$

and the theorem of inversion (12.) may be written thus:

$$\Theta\, b = \Theta\, a, \text{ if } b = a. \tag{52.}$$

The corresponding rules for inverting a non-analogy shew that, in general,

$$\Theta\, b \mp \Theta\, a, \text{ if } b \mp a; \tag{53.}$$

and more particularly, that

$$\Theta\, b < \Theta\, a, \text{ if } b > a, \tag{54.}$$

$$\text{and } \Theta\, b > \Theta\, a, \text{ if } b < a. \tag{55.}$$

It is evident also that

$$\text{if } a' = \Theta\, a, \text{ then } a = \Theta\, a'; \tag{56.}$$

that is, the opposite of the opposite of any proposed relation a is that proposed relation itself; a theorem which may be concisely expressed as follows:

$$\Theta\, (\Theta\, a) = a; \tag{57.}$$

for, as a general rule of notation, when a complex symbol (as here $\Theta\, a$) is substituted in any written sentence (such as here the sentence $a = \Theta\, a'$) instead of a simple symbol (which the symbol a', notwithstanding its accent, is here considered to be), it is expedient, and in most cases necessary, for distinctness, to record and mark this using of a complex as a simple symbol, by some such written warning as the enclosing of the complex symbol in parentheses, or in brackets, or the drawing of a bar across it. However, in the present case, no confusion would be likely to ensue from the omission of such a warning; and we might write at pleasure

$$\Theta\, (\Theta\, a) = a,\ \Theta\, \{\Theta\, a\} = a,\ \Theta\, [\Theta\, a] = a,\ \Theta\, \overline{\Theta\, a} = a, \text{ or simply } \Theta\, \Theta\, a = a. \tag{58.}$$

10. For the purpose of expressing, in a somewhat similar notation, the properties of alternations and combinations of analogies, set forth in the foregoing articles, with some other connected results, and generally for the illustration and development of the conception of ordinal *relations* between moments, it is advantageous to introduce that other connected conception, already alluded to, of *steps* in the progression of time; and to establish this other symbolic definition, or conventional manner of writing, namely,

$$\mathrm{B} = (\mathrm{B} - \mathrm{A}) + \mathrm{A}, \text{ or } \mathrm{B} = a + \mathrm{A} \text{ if } \mathrm{B} - \mathrm{A} = a; \tag{59.}$$

this notation $a + \mathrm{A}$, or $(\mathrm{B} - \mathrm{A}) + \mathrm{A}$, corresponding to the above-mentioned conception of a certain *mental step or act of transition*, which is determined in direction and degree by the ordinal relation a or $\mathrm{B} - \mathrm{A}$, and may, therefore, be called "the step a," or the step $B - A$, and which is such that by making this mental step, or performing this act of transition, we pass, in thought, from the moment A to the moment B, and thus suggest or generate (in thought) the latter from the former, as a mental product or *result* B of the *act* a and of the *object* A. We may also express the same relation between B and A by writing

$$A = (\ominus \, a) + B, \text{ or more simply } A = \ominus \, a + B, \qquad (60.)$$

if we agree to write the sign $\ominus\,a$ without parentheses, as if it were a simple or single symbol, because there is no danger of causing confusion thereby; and if we observe that the notation $A = \ominus \, a + B$ corresponds to the conception of another step, or mental act of transition, $\ominus\,a$, exactly opposite to the former step a, and such that by it we may *return* (in thought) from the moment B to the moment A, and thus may generate A as a result of the act $\ominus\,a$ and of the object B. The mark $+$, in this sort of notation, is interposed, as a *mark of combination*, between the signs of the *act* and the *object*, so as to form a complex sign of the *result*; or, in other words, between the sign of the transition (a or $\ominus$ a) and the sign of the moment (A or B) *from* which that transition is made, so as to express, by a complex sign, (recording the suggestion or generation of the thought,) that other moment (B or A) *to* which this mental transition conducts. And in any transition of this sort, such as that expressed by the *equation* $B = a + A$, we may call (as before) the moment A, *from* which we pass, the *antecedent*, and the moment B, *to* which we pass, the *consequent*, of the ordinal *relation* a, or $B - A$, which suggests and determines the transition. In the particular case when this ordinal relation is one of *identity*, ($a = 0$,) the mental transition or *act* (a or 0) makes no change in the *object* of that act, namely in the *moment* A, but only leads us to *repeat* the thought of that antecedent moment A, perhaps with a new name B; in this case, therefore, the transition may be said to be *null*, or a *null step*, as producing no real alteration in the moment from which it is made. A step *not null*, ($a \neq 0$,) corresponds to a relation of *diversity*, and may be called, by contrast, an *effective* step, because it is an act of thought which really alters its object, namely the moment to which it is applied. An effective step a must be either a *late-making* or an *early-making* step, according as the resultant moment $a + A$ is later or earlier than A; but even a *null* step 0 may be regarded as *relatively late-making*, when compared with an early-making step a, ($0 + A > a + A$, if $a < 0$,) or as *relatively early-making* if compared with a late-making step b; ($0 + A < b + A$, if $b > 0$;) and, in like manner, of two unequal early-making steps, the lesser may be regarded as relatively late-making, while of two unequal late-making steps the lesser step may be considered as relatively early-making. With these conceptions of the *relative effects* of any two steps a and b, we may enunciate in words the non-analogy (44.), ($b > a$, that is, $b + A > a + A$,) by saying that the step b as compared with the step a is *relatively late-making*; and the opposite non-analogy (45.), ($b < a$, that is, $b + A < a + A$,) by saying that the step b as compared with a is *relatively early-making*.

11. After having made any one step a from a proposed moment A to a resulting moment represented (as before) by $a + A$, we may conceive that we next make from this new moment $a + A$ a new step b, and may denote the new result by the new complex symbol $b + (a + A)$; enclosing in parentheses the sign $a + A$ of the *object* of this new *act* of mental transition, or (in other words) the sign of the new antecedent moment, to mark that it is a complex used as a simple symbol; so that, in this notation,

$$\text{if } B - A = a, \text{ and } C - B = b, \text{ then } C = b + (a + A). \tag{61.}$$

It is evident that the *total change* or *total step*, effective or null, from the first moment A to the last moment C, in this successive transition from A to B and from B to C, may be considered as *compounded* of the two successive or *partial steps* a and b, namely the step a from A to B, and the step b from B to C; and that the *ultimate ordinal relation* of C to A may likewise be considered as *compounded* of the two *intermediate* (or suggesting) ordinal relations b and a, namely, the relation b of C to B, and the relation a of B to A; a composition of steps or of relations which may conveniently be denoted, by interposing, as a mark of combination, between the signs of the component steps or of the component ordinal relations, the same mark + which was before employed to combine an act of transition with its object, or an ordinal relation with its antecedent. We shall therefore denote the compound transition from A to C, or the compound relation of C to A, by the complex symbol $b + a$, writing,

$$C - A = b + a, \text{ if } B - A = a, \text{ and } C - B = b, \tag{62.}$$

that is,

$$c = b + a, \text{ if } B = a + A, \ C = b + B, \ C = c + A. \tag{63.}$$

For example, the case of coincidence between the moments A and C, that is, the case when the resulting relation of C to A is the relation of identity, and when therefore the total or compound transition from A to C is null, because the two component or successive steps a and b have been exactly opposite to each other, conducts to the relations,

$$\ominus a + a = 0; \quad b + \ominus b = 0. \tag{64.}$$

In general, the establishment of this new complex mark $\mathrm{b} + \mathrm{a}$, for the compound mental transition from A through B to C, permits us to regard the two written assertions or equations

$$\mathrm{C} = (\mathrm{b} + \mathrm{a}) + \mathrm{A} \text{ and } \mathrm{C} = \mathrm{b} + (\mathrm{a} + \mathrm{A}), \qquad (65.)$$

as expressing the same thing, or as each involving the other; for which reason we are at liberty to omit the parentheses, and may write, more simply, without fear of causing confusion,

$$\mathrm{C} = \mathrm{b} + \mathrm{a} + \mathrm{A}, \text{ if } \mathrm{C} = \mathrm{b} + \mathrm{B}, \text{ and } \mathrm{B} = \mathrm{a} + \mathrm{A}; \qquad (66.)$$

because the complex symbol $\mathrm{b} + \mathrm{a} + \mathrm{A}$ denotes only the one determined moment C, whether it be interpreted by first applying the step a to the moment A, so as to generate another moment denoted by the complex mark $\mathrm{a} + \mathrm{A}$, and afterwards applying to this moment the step denoted by b, or by first combining the steps a and b into one compound step $\mathrm{b} + \mathrm{a}$, and afterwards applying this compound step to the original moment A.

In like manner, if three successive steps a b c have conducted successively (in thought) from A to B, from B to C, and from C to D, and therefore ultimately and upon the whole from A to D, we may consider this total transition from A to D as compounded of the three steps a b c; we may also regard the resulting ordinal relation of D to A as compounded of the three relations c, b, a, namely of the relation c of D to C, the relation b of C to B, and the relation a of B to A; and may denote this compound step or compound relation by the complex symbol $\mathrm{c} + \mathrm{b} + \mathrm{a}$, and the last resulting moment D by the connected symbol $\mathrm{c} + \mathrm{b} + \mathrm{a} + \mathrm{A}$; in such a manner that

$$\left.\begin{array}{l} \mathrm{D} - \mathrm{A} = \mathrm{c} + \mathrm{b} + \mathrm{a}, \text{ and } \mathrm{D} = \mathrm{c} + \mathrm{b} + \mathrm{a} + \mathrm{A}, \\ \text{if } \mathrm{B} - \mathrm{A} = \mathrm{a}, \ \mathrm{C} - \mathrm{B} = \mathrm{b}, \text{ and } \mathrm{D} - \mathrm{C} = \mathrm{c}. \end{array}\right\} \qquad (67.)$$

For example,

$$\left.\begin{array}{l} \mathrm{c} + \Theta\mathrm{a} + \mathrm{a} = \mathrm{c}, \quad \mathrm{c} + \mathrm{b} + \Theta\mathrm{b} = \mathrm{c}, \\ \Theta\mathrm{b} + \mathrm{b} + \mathrm{a} = \mathrm{a}, \quad \mathrm{c} + \Theta\mathrm{c} + \mathrm{a} = \mathrm{a}. \end{array}\right\} \qquad (68.)$$

Remarks of the same kind apply to the composition of more successive steps than three. And we see that in any complex symbol suggested by this sort of composition, such as $\mathrm{c} + \mathrm{b} + \mathrm{a} + \mathrm{A}$, we are at liberty to enclose any two or more successive component symbols, such as c or b or a or A, in parentheses, with their proper combining marks +, and to treat the enclosed set as if they formed only one single symbol; thus,

$$\left.\begin{aligned} \mathrm{c}+\mathrm{b}+\mathrm{a}+\mathrm{A} = \mathrm{c}+\mathrm{b}+(\mathrm{a}+\mathrm{A}) &= \mathrm{c}+(\mathrm{b}+\mathrm{a})+\mathrm{A} \\ &= (\mathrm{c}+\mathrm{b}+\mathrm{a})+\mathrm{A}, \text{ \&c.,} \end{aligned}\right\} \qquad (69.)$$

the notation $\mathrm{c}+(\mathrm{b}+\mathrm{a})+\mathrm{A}$, for example, directing us to begin by combining (in thought) the two steps a and b into one compound step $\mathrm{b}+\mathrm{a}$, and then to apply successively this compound step and the remaining step c to the original moment A; while the notation $(\mathrm{c}+\mathrm{b}+\mathrm{a})+\mathrm{A}$ suggests a previous composition (in thought) of all the three proposed steps a, b, c, into one compound step $\mathrm{c}+\mathrm{b}+\mathrm{a}$, and then the application of this one step to the same original moment. It is clear that all these different processes must conduct to one common result; and generally, that as, by the very meaning and conception of a *compound step*, it may be *applied to any moment* by applying in their proper order its component steps successively, so also may these components be *compounded* successively *with any other step*, as a mode of compounding with that other step the whole original compound.

We may also consider *decomposition* as well as composition of steps, and may propose to deduce either of two components a and b from the other component and from the compound $\mathrm{b}+\mathrm{a}$. For this purpose, it appears from (68.) that we have the relations

$$\mathrm{a} = \Theta\mathrm{b}+\mathrm{c}, \text{ and } \mathrm{b} = \mathrm{c}+\Theta\mathrm{a}, \text{ if } \mathrm{c} = \mathrm{b}+\mathrm{a}; \qquad (70.)$$

observing that a problem of decomposition is plainly a determinate problem, in the sense that if any one component step, such as here the step denoted by $\Theta\mathrm{b}+\mathrm{c}$, or that denoted by $\mathrm{c}+\Theta\mathrm{a}$, has been found to conduct to a given compound c, when combined in a given order with a given component b or a, then no other component a or b, essentially different from the one thus found, can conduct by the same process of composition to the same given compound step. We see then that each of the two components a and b may be deduced from the other, and from the compound c, by compounding with that given compound the opposite of the given component, in a suitable order of composition, which order itself we shall shortly find to be indifferent.

Meanwhile it is important to observe, that though we have agreed, for the sake of conciseness, to omit the parentheses about a complex symbol of the kind $\Theta\mathrm{a}$, when combined with other written signs by the interposed mark +, yet it is in general necessary, if we would avoid confusion, to retain the parentheses, or some such connecting mark or marks, for any complex symbol of a step, when we wish to form, by prefixing the mark of opposition Θ, a symbol for the opposite of that step: for example, the opposite of a compound step $b + a$ must be denoted in some such manner as $\Theta(b + a)$, and not merely by writing $\Theta b + a$. Attending to this remark, we may write

$$\Theta(b + a) = \Theta a + \Theta b, \qquad (71.)$$

because, in order to destroy or undo the effect of the compound step $b + a$, it is sufficient first to apply the step Θb which destroys the effect of the last component step b, and afterwards to destroy the effect of the first component step a by applying its opposite Θa, whatever the two steps denoted by a and b may be. In like manner,

$$\Theta(c + b + a) = \Theta a + \Theta b + \Theta c; \qquad (72.)$$

and similarly for more steps than three.

12. We can now express, in the language of *steps*, several other general theorems, for the most part contained under a different form in the early articles of this Essay.

Thus, the propositions (20.) and (21.), with their reciprocals, may be expressed by saying that if equivalent steps be similarly combined with equivalent steps, whether in the way of composition or of decomposition, they generate equivalent steps; an assertion which may be written thus:

$$\text{if } a' = a, \text{ then } \left.\begin{array}{l} b + a' = b + a, \; a' + b = a + b, \\ b + \Theta a' = b + \Theta a, \; \Theta a' + b = \Theta a + b, \\ \Theta b + a' = \Theta b + a, \; a' + \Theta b = a + \Theta b, \text{ \&c.} \end{array}\right\} \qquad (73.)$$

The proposition (25.) may be considered as expressing, that if two steps be equivalent to the same third step, they are also equivalent to each other; or, that

$$\text{if } a'' = a' \text{ and } a' = a, \text{ then } a'' = a. \qquad (74.)$$

The theorem of alternation of an analogy (11.) may be included in the assertion that in the composition of any two steps, the order of those two components may be changed, without altering the compound step; or that

$$a + b = b + a. \qquad (75.)$$

For, whatever the four moments A B C D may be, which construct any proposed analogy or non-analogy, we may denote the step from A to B by a symbol such as a, and the step from B to D by another symbol b, denoting also the step from A to C by b', and that from C to D by a'; in such a manner that

$$B - A = a, \; D - B = b, \; C - A = b', \; D - C = a'; \qquad (76.)$$

and then the total step from A to D may be denoted either by $b + a$ or by $a' + b'$, according as we conceive the transition performed by passing through B or through C; we have therefore the relation

$$a' + b' = b + a, \qquad (77.)$$

which becomes

$$a + b' = b + a, \qquad (78.)$$

when we establish the analogy

$$D - C = B - A, \text{ that is, } a' = a; \qquad (79.)$$

we see then that if the theorem (75.) be true, we cannot have the analogy (79.) without having also its alternate analogy, namely

$$b = b', \text{ or } D - B = C - A: \qquad (80.)$$

because the compound steps $a + b'$ and $a + b$, with the common second component a, could not be equivalent, if the first components b' and b were not also equivalent to each other. The theorem (75.) includes, therefore, the theorem of alternation.

Reciprocally, from the theorem of alternation considered as known, we can infer the theorem (75.), namely, the indifference of the order of any two successive components a, b, of a compound step: for, whatever those two component steps a and b may be, we can always apply them successively to any one moment A, so as to generate two other moments B and C, and may again apply the step a to C so as to generate a fourth moment D, the moments thus suggested having the properties

$$B = a + A, \ C = b + A, \ D = a + C, \qquad (81.)$$

and being therefore such that

$$D - A = a + b, \ D - C = a = B - A; \qquad (82.)$$

by alternation of which last analogy, between the two pairs of moments A B and C D, we find this other analogy,

$$D - B = C - A = b, \ D = b + B = b + a + A, \qquad (83.)$$

and finally,

$$b + a = D - A = a + b. \qquad (84.)$$

The propositions (22.) (23.) (24.), respecting certain combinations of analogies, are included in the same assertion (75.); which may also, by (71.), be thus expressed,

$$a + b = \Theta\,(\Theta\,a + \Theta\,b), \text{ or, } b + a = \Theta\,(\Theta\,b + \Theta\,a); \qquad (85.)$$

that is, by saying that it comes to the same thing, whether we compound any two steps a and b themselves, or first compound their opposites $\Theta\,a$, $\Theta\,b$, into one compound step $\Theta\,b + \Theta\,a$, and then take the opposite of this. Under this form, the theorem of the possibility of reversing the order of composition may be regarded as evident, whatever the number of the component steps may be; for example, in the case of any three component steps a, b, c, we may regard it as evident that by applying these three steps successively to any moment A, and generating thus three moments B, C, D, we generate moments related to A as A itself is related to those three other moments B′, C′, D′, which are generated from it by applying successively, in the same order, the three respectively opposite steps, $\Theta\,a$, $\Theta\,b$, $\Theta\,c$; that is, if

$$\left.\begin{array}{ll} B = a + A, & B' = \Theta\,a + A, \\ C = b + B, & C' = \Theta\,b + B', \\ D = c + C, & D' = \Theta\,c + C', \end{array}\right\} \qquad (86.)$$

then the sets B′ A B, C′ A C, D′ A D, containing each three moments, form so many continued analogies or equidistant series, such that

$$\left.\begin{array}{l} B - A = A - B' \\ C - A = A - C' \\ D - A = A - D' \end{array}\right\} \qquad (87.)$$

and therefore not only $b + a = \Theta\,(\Theta\,b + \Theta\,a)$, as before, but also

$$c + b + a = \Theta\,(\Theta\,c + \Theta\,b + \Theta\,a), \qquad (88.)$$

that is, by (72.) and (57.),

$$c + b + a = a + b + c; \qquad (89.)$$

and similarly for more steps than three.

The theorem (89.) was contained, indeed, in the reciprocal of the proposition (24.), namely, in the assertion that

$$\left.\begin{array}{rl} \text{if } & D - C = B - A, \\ \text{and } & D' - C = B - A', \\ \text{then } & D' - D = A - A', \end{array}\right\} \qquad (90.)$$

and, therefore, by alternation,

$$\text{D}' - \text{A} = \text{D} - \text{A}'; \qquad (91.)$$

for, whatever the three steps a b c may be, we may always conceive them applied successively to any moment A, so as to generate three other moments B, C, D′, such that

$$\text{B} = \text{a} + \text{A}, \quad \text{C} = \text{b} + \text{B}, \quad \text{D}' = \text{c} + \text{C}, \qquad (92.)$$

and may also conceive two other moments A′ and D such that B C D may be successively generated from A′ by applying the same three steps in the order c, b, a, so that

$$\text{B} = \text{c} + \text{A}', \quad \text{C} = \text{b} + \text{B}, \quad \text{D} = \text{a} + \text{C}; \qquad (93.)$$

and then the two first analogies of the combination (90.) will hold, and, therefore, also the last, together with its alternate (91.); that is, the step from A to D′, compounded of the three steps a b c, is equivalent to the step from A′ to D, compounded of the same three steps in the reverse order c b a.

Since we may thus reverse the order of any three successive steps, and also the order of any two which immediately follow each other, it is easy to see that we may interchange in any manner the order of three successive steps; thus

$$\left.\begin{array}{l} \text{c} + \text{b} + \text{a} = \text{c} + \text{a} + \text{b} = \text{b} + \text{c} + \text{a} \\ = \text{a} + \text{b} + \text{c} = \text{a} + \text{c} + \text{b} = \text{b} + \text{a} + \text{c} \end{array}\right\} \qquad (94.)$$

We might also have proved this theorem (94.), without previously establishing the less general proposition (89.), and in a manner which would extend to any number of component steps; namely, by observing that when any arrangement of component steps is proposed, we may always reserve the first (and by still stronger reason any other) of those steps to be applied the last, and leave the order of the remaining steps unchanged, without altering the whole compound step; because the components which followed, in the proposed arrangement, that one which we now reserve for the last, may be conceived as themselves previously combined into one compound step, and this then interchanged in place with the reserved one, by the theorem respecting the arbitrary order of any two successive steps. In like manner, we might reserve any other step to be the last but one, and any other to be the last but two, and so on; by pursuing which reasoning it becomes manifest that when any number of component steps are applied to any original moment, or compounded with any primary step, their order may be altered at pleasure, without altering the resultant moment, or the whole compounded step: which is, perhaps, the most important and extensive property of the composition of ordinal relations, or steps in the progression of time.

On the Multiples of a given base, or unit-step; and on the Algebraic Addition, Subtraction, Multiplication, and Division, of their determining or multipling Whole Numbers, whether positive, or contra-positive, or null.

13. Let us now apply this general theory of successive and compound steps, from any one moment to any others, or of component and compound ordinal relations between the moments of any arbitrary set, to the case of an equidistant series of moments,

$$\ldots \text{E}'' \; \text{E}' \; \text{E} \; \text{A} \; \text{B} \; \text{B}' \; \text{B}'' \ldots \qquad (29.)$$

constructed so as to satisfy the conditions of a continued analogy,

$$\ldots \text{B}'' - \text{B}' = \text{B}' - \text{B} = \text{B} - \text{A} = \text{A} - \text{E} = \text{E} - \text{E}' = \text{E}' - \text{E}'', \text{ \&c.}; \qquad (30.)$$

and first, for distinctness of conception and of language, let some one moment A of this series be selected as a standard with which all the others are to be compared, and let it be called the *zero-moment;* while the moments B, B′, &c. which *follow* it, in the order of progression of the series, may be distinguished from those other moments E, E′, &c., which *precede* it in that order of progression, by some two contrasted epithets, such as the words *positive* and *contra-positive:* the moment B being called the *positive first,* or the first moment of the series on the positive side of the zero; while in the same plan of nomenclature the moment B′ is the *positive second,* B″ the *positive third,* E the *contra-positive first,* E′ the *contra-positive second,* and so forth. By the nature of the series, as composed of equi-distant moments, or by the conditions (30.), all the positive or *succeeding* moments B B′ &c. may be conceived as *generated* from the zero-moment A, by the continual and successive application of one common step a, and all the contra-positive or *preceding* moments E E′ &c. may be conceived as generated from the same zero-moment A, by the continual and successive application of the opposite step ⊖ a, so that we may write

$$\text{B} = \text{a} + \text{A}, \; \text{B}' = \text{a} + \text{B}, \; \text{B}'' = \text{a} + \text{B}', \text{ \&c.}, \qquad (95.)$$

and

$$\text{E} = \ominus\,\text{a} + \text{A}, \; \text{E}' = \ominus\,\text{a} + \text{E}, \; \text{E}'' = \ominus\,\text{a} + \text{E}', \text{ \&c.}; \qquad (96.)$$

while the standard or zero-moment A itself may be denoted by the complex symbol ⊖ + A, because it may be conceived as generated from itself by applying the null step

0. Hence, by the theory of compound steps, we have expressions of the following sort for all the several moments of the equi-distant series (29.):

$$\left.\begin{array}{l} \dots\dots\dots\dots \\ \mathrm{E}'' = \Theta\,\mathrm{a} + \Theta\,\mathrm{a} + \Theta\,\mathrm{a} + \mathrm{A}, \\ \mathrm{E}' = \Theta\,\mathrm{a} + \Theta\,\mathrm{a} + \mathrm{A}, \\ \mathrm{E} = \Theta\,\mathrm{a} + \mathrm{A}, \\ \mathrm{A} = 0 + \mathrm{A}, \\ \mathrm{B} = \mathrm{a} + \mathrm{A}, \\ \mathrm{B}' = \mathrm{a} + \mathrm{a} + \mathrm{A}, \\ \mathrm{B}'' = \mathrm{a} + \mathrm{a} + \mathrm{a} + \mathrm{A}, \\ \dots\dots\dots\dots \end{array}\right\} \qquad (97.)$$

with corresponding expressions for their several ordinal relations to the one standard moment A, or for the acts of transition which are made in passing from A to them, namely:

$$\left.\begin{array}{l} \dots\dots\dots\dots \\ \mathrm{E}'' - \mathrm{A} = \Theta\,\mathrm{a} + \Theta\,\mathrm{a} + \Theta\,\mathrm{a}, \\ \mathrm{E}' - \mathrm{A} = \Theta\,\mathrm{a} + \Theta\,\mathrm{a}, \\ \mathrm{E} - \mathrm{A} = \Theta\,\mathrm{a}, \\ \mathrm{A} - \mathrm{A} = 0, \\ \mathrm{B} - \mathrm{A} = \mathrm{a}, \\ \mathrm{B}' - \mathrm{A} = \mathrm{a} + \mathrm{a}, \\ \mathrm{B}'' - \mathrm{A} = \mathrm{a} + \mathrm{a} + \mathrm{a}, \\ \quad \&\mathrm{c}. \end{array}\right\} \qquad (98.)$$

The simple or compound step, a, or a + a, &c., from the zero-moment A to any positive moment B or B′ &c. of the series, may be called a *positive step*; and the opposite simple or compound step, Θ a, or Θ a + Θ a, &c., from the same zero-moment A to any contra-positive moment E or E′, &c., of the series, may be called a *contra-positive step*; while the null step 0, from the zero-moment A to itself, may be called, by analogy of language, the *zero-step*. The original step a is supposed to be an effective step, and not a null one, since otherwise the whole series of moments (97.) would reduce themselves to the one original moment A; but it may be either a late-making or an early-making step, according as the (mental) order of progression of that series is from earlier to later, or from later to earlier moments. And the whole series or system of steps (98.), simple or compound, positive or contra-positive, effective or null, which serve to generate the several moments of the equi-distant series (29.) or (97.) from the original or standard moment A, may be regarded as a *system of steps generated from the original step* a, by a *system of acts* of generation which are all of one common kind; each step having therefore a certain *relation* of its own to that original step, and these relations having all a general resemblance to each other, so that they may be conceived as composing a certain *system of relations*, having all one common character. To mark this *common generation* of the system of steps (98.) from the one original step a, and their *common relation* thereto, we may call them all by the common name of *multiples* of that original step, and may say that they are or may be (mentally) formed by *multipling* that common *base*, or *unit-step*, a; distinguishing, however, these several multiples among themselves by peculiar or special names, which shall serve to mark the peculiar relation of any one multiple to the base, or the special act of multipling by which it may be conceived to be generated therefrom.

Thus, the null step, or zero-step, 0, which conducts to the zero-moment A, may be called, according to this way of conceiving it, the *zero multiple* of the original step a; and the positive (effective) steps, simple or compound, a, $\mathrm{a}+\mathrm{a}$, $\mathrm{a}+\mathrm{a}+\mathrm{a}$, &c., may be called by the general name of *positive multiples* of a, and may be distinguished by the special ordinal names of *first, second, third*, &c., so that the original step a is, in this view, its own first positive multiple; and finally, the contra-positive (but effective) steps, simple or compound, namely, $\Theta\,\mathrm{a}$, $\Theta\,\mathrm{a}+\Theta\,\mathrm{a}$, $\Theta\,\mathrm{a}+\Theta\,\mathrm{a}+\Theta\,\mathrm{a}$, &c., may be called the *first contra-positive multiple* of a, the *second contra-positive multiple* of the same original step a, and so forth. Some particular multiples have particular and familiar names; for example, the second positive multiple of a step may also be called the *double* of that step, and the third positive multiple may be called familiarly the *triple*. In general, the original step a may be called (as we just now agreed) the common *base* (or *unit*) of all these several multiples; and the ordinal name or number, (such as zero, or positive first, or contra-positive second,) which serves as a special mark to distinguish some one of these multiples from every other, in the general series of such multiples (98.), may be called the *determining ordinal*: so that any one multiple step is sufficiently described, when we mention its base and its determining ordinal. In conformity with this conception of the series of steps (98.,) as a *series of multiples of the base* a, we may denote them by the following series of written symbols,

$$\ldots\ldots\ 3\,\Theta\,\mathrm{a},\ 2\,\Theta\,\mathrm{a},\ 1\,\Theta\,\mathrm{a},\ 0\,\mathrm{a},\ 1\,\mathrm{a},\ 2\,\mathrm{a},\ 3\,\mathrm{a},\ \ldots \qquad (99.)$$

and may denote the moments themselves of the equi-distant series (29.) or (97.) by the symbols,

$$\left.\begin{array}{l} \ldots\ldots \\ \mathrm{E}'' = 3\,\Theta\,\mathrm{a} + \mathrm{A}, \\ \mathrm{E}' = 2\,\Theta\,\mathrm{a} + \mathrm{A}, \\ \mathrm{E} = 1\,\Theta\,\mathrm{a} + \mathrm{A}, \\ \mathrm{A} = 0\,\mathrm{a} + \mathrm{A}, \\ \mathrm{B} = 1\,\mathrm{a} + \mathrm{A}, \\ \mathrm{B}' = 2\,\mathrm{a} + \mathrm{A}, \\ \mathrm{B}'' = 3\,\mathrm{a} + \mathrm{A}, \\ \&c.\,; \end{array}\right\} \qquad (100.)$$

in which

$$0\,\mathrm{a} = 0, \qquad (101.)$$

and

$$\left.\begin{array}{ll} 1\,\mathrm{a} = \mathrm{a}, & 1\,\Theta\,\mathrm{a} = \Theta\,\mathrm{a}, \\ 2\,\mathrm{a} = \mathrm{a} + \mathrm{a}, & 2\,\Theta\,\mathrm{a} = \Theta\,\mathrm{a} + \Theta\,\mathrm{a}, \\ 3\,\mathrm{a} = \mathrm{a} + \mathrm{a} + \mathrm{a}, & 3\,\Theta\,\mathrm{a} = \Theta\,\mathrm{a} + \Theta\,\mathrm{a} + \Theta\,\mathrm{a}, \\ \&c., & \&c. \end{array}\right\} \qquad (102.)$$

The written sign 0 in $0\,\mathrm{a}$ is here equivalent to the spoken name *zero*, as the determining ordinal of the null step from A to A, which step was itself also denoted before by the same character 0, and is here considered as the *zero-multiple* of the base a; while the written signs 1, 2, 3, &c., in the symbols of the positive multiples $1\,\mathrm{a}$, $2\,\mathrm{a}$, $3\,\mathrm{a}$, &c., correspond to and denote the determining positive ordinals, or the spoken names *first positive, second positive, third positive*, &c.; and, finally, the remaining written signs $1\,\Theta$, $2\,\Theta$, $3\,\Theta$, &c., which are combined with the written sign of the base a, in the symbols of the contra-positive multiples $1\,\Theta\,\mathrm{a}$, $2\,\Theta\,\mathrm{a}$, $3\,\Theta\,\mathrm{a}$, &c., correspond to and denote the determining ordinal names of those contra-positive multiples, that is, they correspond to the spoken names, *first contra-positive, second contra-positive, third contra-positive*, &c.: so that the series of signs of multiple steps (99.), is formed by combining the symbol of the base a with the following series of ordinal symbols,

$$\ldots 3\,\Theta,\ 2\,\Theta,\ 1\,\Theta,\ 0,\ 1,\ 2,\ 3,\ \&c. \qquad (103.)$$

We may also conceive this last series of signs as equivalent, not to *ordinal* names, such as the numeral word *first*, but to *cardinal* names, such as the numeral word *one*; or more fully, *positive cardinals*, *contra-positive cardinals*, and the *null cardinal* (or number *none*); namely, the system of all possible answers to the following complex question: "*Have any* effective steps (equivalent or opposite to the given base a) been made (from the standard moment A), and if any, then *How many*, and *In which direction?*" In this view, $3\,\Theta$ is a written sign of the *cardinal* name or number *contra-positive three,* as a possible answer to the foregoing general question; and it implies, when prefixed to the sign of the base a, in the complex written sign 3 Θ a of the corresponding multiple step, that this multiple step has been formed, (as already shown in the equations (102.),) by making three steps equal to the base a in length, but in the direction opposite thereto. Again, the mark 1 may be regarded as a written sign of the cardinal number *positive one,* and 1 a denotes (in this view) the step formed by making one such step as a, and in the same direction, that is, (as before,) the original step a itself; and 0 denotes the cardinal number *none,* so that 0 a is (as before) a symbol for the null step from A to A, which step we have also marked before by the simple symbol 0, and which is here considered as formed by making *no* effective step like a. In general, this view of the numeral signs (103.), as denoting *cardinal* numbers, conducts to the same ultimate interpretations of the symbols (99.), for the steps of the series (98.), as the former view, which regarded those signs (103.) as denoting *ordinal* numbers.

If we adopt the latter view of those numeral signs (103.), which we shall call by the common name of *whole* (or *integer*) *numbers,* (as distinguished from certain broken or fractional numbers to be considered afterwards,) we may conveniently continue to use the word *multiple* (occasionally) as a verb active, and may speak of the several multiple steps of the series (98.), or (99.), as formed from the base a, by *multipling that base by the several whole* (cardinal) *numbers:* because every multiple step may be conceived as generated (in thought) from the base, by a certain mental act, of which the cardinal number is the mark. Thus we may describe the multiple step 3 Θ a, (which is, in the ordinal view, the third contra-positive multiple of a,) as formed from the base a by *multipling it by contra-positive three.* Some particular acts of multipling have familiar and special names, and we may speak (for instance) of *doubling* or *tripling* a step, instead of describing that step as being multipled by positive two, or by positive three. In general, to distinguish more clearly, in the written symbol of a multiple step, between the base and the determining number (ordinal or cardinal), and to indicate more fully the performance of that mental act (directed by the number) which generates the multiple from the base, the mark × may be inserted between the sign of the base, and the sign of the number; and thus we may denote the series of multiple steps (99.) by the following fuller symbols,

$$\ldots\ 3\,\Theta \times a,\ 2\,\Theta \times a,\ 1\,\Theta \times a,\ 0 \times a,\ 1 \times a,\ 2 \times a,\ 3 \times a,\ \&c., \qquad (104.)$$

and which 1 × a (for example) denotes the original step a itself, and 2 × a represents the double of that original step.

It is manifest that in this notation

$$\left. \begin{aligned} n\,\Theta \times a &= n \times \Theta\, a = \Theta\,(n \times a) = \Theta\,(n\,\Theta \times \Theta\, a), \\ \text{and } n \times a &= n\,\Theta \times \Theta\, a = \Theta\,(n\,\Theta \times a) = \Theta\,(n \times \Theta\, a), \end{aligned} \right\} \tag{105.}$$

if n denote any one of the positive numbers 1, 2, 3, &c. and if $n\,\Theta$ denote the corresponding contra-positive number, $1\,\Theta$, $2\,\Theta$, $3\,\Theta$, &c.; for example, the equation $2\,\Theta \times a = 2 \times \Theta\, a$ is true, because it expresses that the second contra-positive multiple of the base a is the same step as the second positive multiple of the opposite base or step $\Theta\, a$, the latter multiple being derived from this opposite base by merely doubling its length without reversing its direction, while the former is derived from the original base a itself by both reversing it in direction and doubling it in length, so that both processes conduct to the one common compound step, $\Theta\, a + \Theta\, a$. In like manner the equation $2 \times a = 2\,\Theta \times \Theta\, a$ is true, because by first reversing the direction of the original step a, and then taking the reversed step $\Theta\, a$ as a new base, and forming the second contra-positive multiple of it, which is done by reversing and doubling, and which is the process of generation expressed by the symbol $2\,\Theta \times \Theta\, a$, we form in the end the same compound step, $a + a$, as if we had merely doubled a. We may also conveniently annex the mark of opposition Θ, at the left hand, to the symbol of any whole number, n or $n\,\Theta$ or 0, in order to form a symbol of its opposite number, $n\,\Theta$, n, or 0; and thus may write

$$\Theta\, n = n\,\Theta, \quad \Theta\,(n\,\Theta) = n, \quad \Theta\, 0 = 0; \tag{106.}$$

if we still denote by n any positive whole number, and if we call two whole numbers *opposites* of each other, when they are the determining or multipling numbers of two opposite multiple steps.

14. Two or more multiples such as $\mu \times a$, $\nu \times a$, $\xi \times a$, of the same base a, may be compounded as *successive steps* with each other, and the resulting or compound step will manifestly be itself some multiple, such as $\omega \times a$, of the same common base a; the signs μ, ν, ξ, denoting here any arbitrary whole numbers, whether positive, or contra-positive, or null, and ω denoting another whole number, namely the determining number of the compound multiple step, which must evidently depend on the determining numbers $\mu\ \nu\ \xi$ of the component multiple steps, and on those alone, according to some general law of dependence. This law may conveniently be denoted, in writing, by the same mark of combination + which has been employed already to form the complex symbol of the compound step itself, considered as depending on the component steps; that is, we may agree to write

$$\omega = \nu + \mu, \text{ when } \omega \times a = (\nu \times a) + (\mu \times a), \qquad (107.)$$

and

$$\omega = \xi + \nu + \mu, \text{ when } \omega \times a = (\xi \times a) + (\nu \times a) + (\mu \times a), \qquad (108.)$$

together with other similar expressions for the case of more component steps than three. In this notation,

$$\left.\begin{array}{c} (\nu \times a) + (\mu \times a) = (\nu + \mu) \times a, \\ (\xi \times a) + (\nu \times a) + (\mu \times a) = (\xi + \nu + \mu) \times a, \\ \&c. \end{array}\right\} \qquad (109.)$$

whatever the whole numbers $\mu\ \nu\ \xi$ may be; equations which are to be regarded here as true by definition, and as only serving to explain the meaning attributed to such complex signs as $\nu + \mu$, or $\xi + \nu + \mu$, when $\mu\ \nu\ \xi$ are any symbols of whole numbers: although when we farther assert that the equations (109.) are true independently of the base or unit-step a, so that symbols of the form $\nu + \mu$ or $\xi + \nu + \mu$ denote whole numbers independent of that base, we express in a new way a theorem which we had before assumed to be evidently true, as an axiom and not a definition, respecting the composition of multiple steps.

In the particular case when the whole numbers denoted by $\mu\ \nu\ \xi$ are positive, the law of composition of those numbers expressed by the notation $\nu + \mu$ or $\xi + \nu + \mu$, as explained by the equations (109.), is easily seen to be the law called *addition* of numbers (that is of quotities) in elementary arithmetic; and the quotity of the compound or resulting whole number is the arithmetical *sum* of the quotities of the component numbers, this arithmetical *sum* being the answer to the question, *How many* things or thoughts does a total group contain, if it be composed of *partial groups* of which the quotities are given, namely the numbers to be arithmetically *added.* For example, since $(3 \times a) + (2 \times a)$ is the symbol for the total or compound multiple step composed of the double and the triple of the base a, it must denote the quintuple or fifth positive multiple of that base, namely $5 \times a$; and since we have agreed to write

$$(3 \times a) + (2 \times a) = (3 + 2) \times a,$$

we must interpret the complex symbol $3 + 2$ as equivalent to the simple symbol 5; in seeking for which latter number *five*, we *added*, in the arithmetical sense, the given component numbers *two* and *three* together, that is, we formed their arithmetical *sum*, by considering how many steps are contained in a total group of steps, if the component or partial groups contain two steps and three steps respectively. In like manner, if we admit in arithmetic the idea of the cardinal number *none*, as one of the possible answers to the fundamental question *How many*, the rules of the arithmetical addition of this number to others, and of others to it, and the properties of the arithmetical sums thus composed, agree with the rules and properties of such combinations as $0 + \mu$, $\xi + \nu + 0$, explained by the equations (109.), when the whole numbers, μ, ν, ξ, are positive; we shall, therefore, not clash in our enlarged phraseology with the language of elementary arithmetic, respecting the addition of numbers regarded as answers to the question *How many*, if we now establish, as a definition, in the more extensive *Science of Pure Time*, that any combination of whole numbers $\mu\ \nu\ \xi$, of the form $\nu + \mu$, or $\xi + \nu + \mu$, interpreted so as to satisfy the equations (109.), is the *sum* of those whole numbers, and is composed by *adding* them together, whether they be positive, or contra-positive, or null. But as a mark that these words *sum* and *adding* are used in ALGEBRA (as the general Science of Pure Time), in a more extensive sense than that in which *Arithmetic* (as the science of counting) employs them, we may, more fully, call $\nu + \mu$ the *algebraic sum* of the whole numbers μ and ν, and say that it is formed by the operation of *algebraically adding* them together, ν to μ.

In general, we may extend the arithmetical names of *sum* and *addition* to every algebraical combination of the class marked by the sign +, and may give to that combining sign the arithmetical name of *Plus*; although in Algebra the idea of *more*, (originally implied by *plus*,) is only occasionally and accidentally involved in the conception of such combinations. For example, the written symbol $\mathrm{b} + \mathrm{a}$, by which we have already denoted the compound step formed by *compounding* the step b as a successive step with the step a, may be expressed in words by the phrase "a plus b," (such written algebraic expressions as these being read from right to left,) or "the algebraic sum of the steps a and b;" and this algebraic sum or compound step $\mathrm{b} + \mathrm{a}$ may be said to be formed by "algebraically adding b to a:" although this compound step is only occasionally and accidentally greater in length than its components, being necessarily shorter than one of them, when they are both effective steps with directions opposite to each other. Even the *application* of a step a to a moment A, so as to generate another moment $\mathrm{a} + \mathrm{A}$, may not improperly be called (by the same analogy of language) the *algebraic addition* of the step to the moment, and the moment generated thereby may be called their *algebraic sum*, or "the original moment *plus* the step;" though in this sort of combination the moment and the step to be combined are not even homogeneous with each other.

With respect to the process of calculation of an algebraic sum of whole numbers, the following rules are evident consequences of what has been already shown respecting the composition of steps. In the first place, the numbers to be added may be added in any arbitrary order; that is,

$$\left.\begin{array}{l} \nu+\mu=\mu+\nu, \\ \xi+\nu+\mu=\mu+\xi+\nu= \&c., \\ \quad\&c.; \end{array}\right\} \qquad (110.)$$

we may therefore collect the positive numbers into one algebraical sum, and the contra-positive into another, and then add these two partial sums to find the total sum, omitting (if it anywhere occur) the number None or Zero, as not capable of altering the result. In the next place, positive numbers are algebraically added to each other, by arithmetically adding the corresponding arithmetical numbers or quotities, and considering the result as a positive number; thus positive two and positive three, when added, give positive five: and contra-positive numbers, in like manner, are algebraically added to each other, by arithmetically adding their quotities, and considering the result as a contra-positive number; thus, contra-positive two and contra-positive three have contra-positive five for their algebraic sum. In the third place, a positive number and a contra-positive, when the quotity of the positive exceeds that of the contra-positive, give a positive algebraic sum, in which the quotity is equal to that excess; thus positive five added to contra-positive three, gives positive two for the algebraic sum: and similarly, a positive number and a contra-positive number, if the quotity of the contra-positive exceed that of the positive, give a contra-positive algebraic sum, with a quotity equal to the excess; for example, if we add positive three to contra-positive five, we get contra-positive two for the result. Finally, a positive number and a contra-positive, with equal quotities, (such as positive three and contra-positive three,) destroy each other by addition; that is, they generate as their algebraic sum the number None or Zero.

It is unnecessary to dwell on the algebraical operation of *decomposition of multiple steps*, and consequently of whole or *multipling numbers*, which corresponds to and includes the operation of arithmetical *subtraction;* since it follows manifestly from the foregoing articles of this Essay, that the decomposition of numbers (like that of steps) can always be performed by *compounding* with the given compound number (that is, by algebraically *adding* thereto) the *opposite* or opposites of the given component or components: the number or numbers proposed to be subtracted are therefore either to be neglected if they be null, since in that case they have no effect, or else to be changed from positive to contra-positive, or from contra-positive to positive, (their quotities being preserved,) and then added (algebraically) in this altered state. Thus, positive five is subtracted algebraically from positive two by adding contra-positive five, and the result is contra-positive three; that is, the given step $2 \times a$ or $2\,a$ may be decomposed into two others, of which the given component step $5 \times a$ is one, and the sought component step $3 \ominus a$ is the other.

15. Any multiple step $\mu\, a$ may be treated as a new base, or new unit-step; and thus we may generate from it a new system of multiple steps. It is evident that these multiples of a multiple of a step are themselves also multiples of that step; that is, if we first multiple a given base or unit-step a by any whole number μ, and then again multiple the result $\mu \times a$ by any other whole number ν, the final result $\nu \times (\mu \times a)$ will necessary be of the form $\omega \times a$, ω being another whole number. It is easy also to see that the new multipling number, such as ω, of the new or derived multiple, must depend on the old or given multipling numbers, such as μ and ν, and on those alone; and the law of its dependence on them may be conveniently expressed by the same mark of combination $\times$ which we have already used to combine any multipling number with its base; so that we may agree to write

$$\omega = \nu \times \mu, \text{ when } \omega \times a = \nu \times (\mu \times a). \qquad (111.)$$

With this definition of the effect of the combining sign $\times$, when interposed between the signs of two whole numbers, we may write

$$\nu \times (\mu \times a) = (\nu \times \mu) \times a = \nu \times \mu \times a, \qquad (112.)$$

omitting the parentheses as unnecessary; because, although their absence permits us to interpret the complex symbol $\nu \times \mu \times a$ either as $\nu \times (\mu \times a)$ or as $(\nu \times \mu) \times a$, yet both the processes of combination thus denoted conduct to one common result, or ultimate multiple step. (Compare article 11.)

When μ and ν are positive numbers, the law of combination expressed by the notation $\nu \times \mu$, as above explained, is easily seen to be that which is called *Multiplication* in elementary Arithmetic, namely, the arithmetical addition of a given number ν of equal quotities μ; and the resulting quotity $\nu \times \mu$ is the arithmetical *product* of the numbers to be combined, or the product of μ multiplied by ν: thus we must, by the definition (112.), interpret 3×2 as denoting the positive number 6, because $3 \times (2 \times a) = 6 \times a$, the triple of the double of any step a being the sextuple of that step; and the quotity 6 is, for the same reason, the arithmetical product of 2 multiplied by 3, in the sense of being the answer to the question, How many things or thoughts (in this case, steps) are contained in a total group, if that total group be composed of 3 partial groups, and if 2 such things or thoughts be contained in each of these? From this analogy to arithmetic, we may in general call $\nu \times \mu$ the *product*, or (more fully) the *algebraic product*, of the whole numbers μ and ν, whether these, which we may call the *factors* of the product, be positive, or contra-positive, or null; and may speak of the process of combination of those numbers, as the *multipling*, or (more fully) the *algebraic multipling* of μ by ν: reserving still the more familiar arithmetical word "multiplying" to be used in algebra in a more general sense, which includes the operation of multipling, and which there will soon be occasion to explain.

In like manner, three or more whole numbers, μ, ν, ξ, may be used successively to multiple a given step or one another, and so to generate a new derived multiple of the original step or number; thus, we may write

$$\xi \times \{\nu \times (\mu \times \mathrm{a})\} = \xi \times \{(\nu \times \mu) \times \mathrm{a}\} = (\xi \times \nu \times \mu) \times \mathrm{a}, \qquad (113.)$$

the symbol $\xi \times \nu \times \mu$ denoting here a new whole number, which may be called the algebraic *product* of the *three* whole numbers μ, ν, ξ, those numbers themselves being called the *factors* of this product. With respect to the actual processes of such *multipling*, or the rules for forming such algebraic *products* of whole numbers, (whether positive, or contra-positive, or null,) it is sufficient to observe that the product is evidently null if any one of the factors be null, but that otherwise the product is contra-positive or positive, according as there is or is not an odd number (such as one, or three, or five, &c.) of contra-positive factors, because the direction of a step is not changed, or is restored, when it is either not reversed at all, or reversed an even number of times; and that, in every case, the quotity of the algebraic product is the arithmetical product of the quotities of the factors. Hence, by the properties of arithmetical products, or by the principles of the present essay, we see that in forming an algebraical product the order of the factors may be altered in any manner without altering the result, so that

$$\nu \times \mu = \mu \times \nu, \quad \xi \times \nu \times \mu = \mu \times \xi \times \nu = \&c., \&c.; \qquad (114.)$$

and that any one of the factors may be decomposed in any manner into algebraical parts or component whole numbers, according to the rules of algebraic addition and subtraction of whole numbers, and each part separately combined as a factor with the other factors to form a partial product, and then these partial products algebraically added together, and that the result will be the total product; that is,

$$\left.\begin{aligned} (\nu' + \nu) \times \mu &= (\nu' \times \mu) + (\nu \times \mu), \\ \nu \times (\mu' + \mu) &= (\nu \times \mu') + (\nu \times \mu), \ \&c. \end{aligned}\right\} \qquad (115.)$$

Again, we saw that if a factor μ be null, the product is then null also,

$$\nu \times 0 = 0; \qquad (116.)$$

because the multiples of a null multiple step are all themselves null steps. But if, in a product of two whole numbers, $\nu \times \mu$, the first factor μ (with which by (114.) the second factor ν may be interchanged) be given, and effective, that is, if it be any given positive or contra-positive whole number, ($\mu \neq 0$,) then its several multiples, or the products of the form $\nu \times \mu$, form an indefinite series of whole numbers,

$$\ldots\ 3\,\Theta \times \mu,\ 2\,\Theta \times \mu,\ 1\,\Theta \times \mu,\ 0 \times \mu,\ 1 \times \mu,\ 2 \times \mu,\ 3 \times \mu,\ \ldots \qquad (117.)$$

such that any proposed whole number ω, whatever, must be either a number of this series, or else included between two successive numbers of it, such as $\nu \times \mu$ and $(1+\nu) \times \mu$, being on the positive side of one of them, and on the contra-positive side of the other, in the complete series of whole numbers (103.). In the one case, we can satisfy the equation

$$\omega = \nu \times \mu, \text{ or, } \Theta\,(\nu \times \mu) + \omega = 0, \qquad (118.)$$

by a suitable choice of the whole number ν; in the other case, we cannot indeed do this, but we can choose a whole number ν, such that

$$\omega = \rho + (\nu \times \mu), \text{ or, } \Theta(\nu \times \mu) + \omega = \rho, \qquad (119.)$$

ρ being a whole number which lies between 0 and μ in the general series of whole numbers (103.), and which therefore has a quotity less than the quotity of that given first factor μ, and is positive or contra-positive according as μ is positive or contra-positive. In each case, we may be said (by analogy to arithmetical division) to have *algebraically divided* (or rather *measured*), accurately or approximately, the whole number ω by the whole number μ, and to have found a whole number ν which is either the *accurate quotient* (or *measure*), as in the case (118.), or else the *next preceding integer*, as in the other case (119.); in which last case the whole number ρ may be called the *remainder* of the division (or of the *measuring*). In this second case, namely, when it is impossible to perform the division, or the *measuring*, exactly, in whole numbers, because the proposed *dividend*, or *mensurand*, ω, is not contained among the series (117.) of multiples of the proposed *divisor*, or *measurer*, μ, we may choose to consider as the approximate integer *quotient*, or *measure*, the *next succeeding* whole number $1 + \nu$, instead of the next preceding whole number ν; and then we shall have a different *remainder*, $\Theta\,\mu + \rho$, such that

$$\omega = (\Theta\mu + \rho) + (\overline{1 + \nu} \times \mu), \qquad (120.)$$

which new remainder $\Theta\mu+\rho$ has still a quotity less than that of μ, but lies between 0 and $\Theta\mu$, instead of lying (like ρ) between 0 and μ, in the general series of whole numbers (103.), and is therefore contra-positive if μ be positive, or positive if μ be contra-positive. With respect to the actual process of calculation, for discovering whether a proposed algebraical division (or measuring), of one whole number by another, conducts to an accurate integer quotient, or only to two approximate integer quotients, a next preceding and a next succeeding, with positive and contra-positive remainders; and for actually finding the names of these several quotients and remainders, or their several special places in the general series of whole numbers: this algebraical process differs only by some slight and obvious modifications (on which it is unnecessary here to dwell,) from the elementary arithmetical operation of dividing one quotity by another; that is, the operation of determining what multiple the one is of the other, or between what two successive multiples it is contained. Thus, having decomposed by arithmetical division the quotity 8 into the arithmetical sum of 1×5 and 3, and having found that it falls short by 2 of the arithmetical product 2×5, we may easily infer from hence that the algebraic whole number *contra-positive eight* can be only approximately measured (in whole numbers), as a mensurand, by the measurer *positive five*; the next succeeding integer quotient or measure being *contra-positive one*, with *contra-positive three* for remainder, and the next preceding integer quotient or measure being *contra-positive two*, with *positive two* as the remainder. It is easy also to see that this algebraic measuring of one whole number by another, corresponds to the accurate or approximate measuring of one step by another. And in like manner may all other arithmetical operations and reasonings upon quotities be generalised in Algebra, by the consideration of multiple steps, and of their connected positive and contra-positive and null whole numbers.

On the Sub-multiples and Fractions of any given Step in the Progression of Time; on the Algebraic Addition, Subtraction, Multiplication, and Division, of Reciprocal and Fractional Numbers, positive and contra-positive; and on the impossible or indeterminate act of sub-multipling or dividing by zero.

16. We have seen that from the thought of any one step a, as a base or unit-step, we can pass to the thought of a series or system of multiples of that base, namely, the series (98.) or (99.) or (104.), having each a certain relation of its own

to the base, as such or such a particular multiple thereof, or as mentally generated from that base by such or such a particular act of multipling; and that every such particular relation, and every such particular act of multipling, may be distinguished from all such other relations, and from all such other acts, in the entire series or system of these relations, and in the entire system of these acts of multipling, by its own special or determining whole number, whether ordinal or cardinal, and whether positive, or contra-positive, or null. Now every such relation or act must be conceived to have a certain inverse or reciprocal, by which we may, in thought, connect the base with the multiple, and return to the former from the latter: and, generally, the conception of passing (in thought) from a base or unit-step to any one of its multiples, or of returning from the multiple to the base, is included in the more comprehensive conception of passing from any one such multiple to any other; that is, from any one step to any other step *commensurable* therewith, two steps being said to be *commensurable* with each other when they are multiples of one common base or unit-step, because they have then that common base or unit for their *common measurer*. The base, when thus compared with one of its own multiples, may be called a *sub-multiple* thereof; and, more particularly, we may call it the "second positive sub-multiple" of its own second positive multiple, the "first contra-positive sub-multiple" of its own first contra-positive multiple, and so forth; retaining always, to distinguish any one sub-multiple, the determining ordinal of the multiple to which it corresponds: and the act of returning from a multiple to the base, may be called an act of *sub-multipling* or (more fully) of sub-multipling *by* the same determining cardinal number by which the base had been multipled before; for example, we may return to the base from its second contra-positive multiple, by an act of thought which may be called sub-multipling by contra-positive two. Some particular sub-multiples, and acts of sub-multipling, have particular and familiar names; thus, the second positive sub-multiple of any given step, and the act of sub-multipling a given step by positive two, may be more familiarly described as the *half* of that given step, and as the act of *halving* it. And the more comprehensive conception above mentioned, of the act of passing from any one step b to any other step c commensurable therewith, or from any one to any other multiple of one common measure, or base, or unit-step a, may evidently be resolved into the foregoing conceptions of the acts of multipling and sub-multipling; since we can always pass first by an act of sub-multipling from the given step b, considered as a multiple of the base a, to that base a itself, as an auxiliary or intermediate thought, and then proceed, by an act of multipling, from this auxiliary thought or step, to its other multiple c. Any one step c may therefore be considered as a multiple of a sub-multiple of any other step b, if those two steps be commensurable; and the act of passing from the one to the other is an act compounded of sub-multipling and multipling.

Now, all acts thus compounded, besides the acts of multipling and sub-multipling themselves, (and other acts, to be considered afterwards, which may be regarded as of the same kind with these, being connected with them by certain intimate relations, and by one common character,) may be classed in algebra under the general name of *multiplying acts*, or acts of *algebraic multiplication;* the *object* on which any such *act* operates being called the *multiplicand*, and the *result* being called the *product;* while the *distinctive thought or sign* of such an act is called the *algebraic multiplier*, or *multiplying number:* whatever this distinctive thought or sign may be, that is, whatever conceived, or spoken, or written *specific rule* it may involve, for specifying one particular act of multiplication, and for distinguishing it from every other. The relation of an algebraic product to its algebraic multiplicand may be called, in general, *ratio*, or *algebraic ratio;* but the particular ratio of any one particular product to its own particular multiplicand, depends on the particular act of multiplication by which the one may be generated from the other: the *number* which specifies the *act* of multiplication, serves therefore also to specify the resulting *ratio*, and every number may be viewed either as the *mark of a ratio*, or as the *mark of a multiplication*, according as we conceive ourselves to be *analytically examining* a product already formed, or *synthetically generating* that product.

We have already considered that series or system of *algebraic integers*, or *whole numbers*, (positive, contra-positive, or null,) which mark the several possible ratios of all multiple steps to their base, and the several acts of multiplication by which the former may be generated from the latter; namely all those several acts which we have included under the common head of *multipling*. The inverse or reciprocal acts of *sub-multipling*, which we must now consider, and which we have agreed to regard as comprehended under the more general head of *multiplication*, conduct to a new class of multiplying numbers, which we may call *reciprocals of whole numbers*, or, more concisely, *reciprocal numbers;* and to a corresponding class of ratios, which we may call *reciprocals of integer ratios*. And the more comprehensive conception of the act of passing from one to another of any two commensurable steps, conducts to a correspondingly extensive class of multiplying acts, and therefore also of multiplying numbers, and of ratios, which we may call *acts of fractioning*, and *fractional numbers*, or *fractional ratios;* while the *product* of any such act of fractioning, or of multiplying by any such fractional number, that is, the *generated step* which is any multiple of any sub-multiple of any proposed step or *multiplicand*, may be called a *fraction* of that step, or of that multiplicand. A fractional number may therefore always be determined, in thought and in expression, by *two whole numbers,* namely the sub-multipling number, called also the *denominator,* and the multipling number, called also the *numerator,* (of the fraction or fractional number,) which mark the two successive or component acts that make up the complex act of fractioning. Hence also the reciprocal number, or reciprocal of any proposed whole number, which marks the act of multiplication conceived to be equivalent to the act of sub-multipling by that whole number, coincides with the fractional number which has the same whole number for its denominator, and the number 1 for its numerator, because a step is not altered when it is multipled by positive one. And any whole number itself, considered as the mark of any special act of multipling, may be changed to a fractional number with positive one for its denominator, and with the proposed whole number for its numerator; since such a fractional number, considered as the mark of a special act of multiplication, is only the complex mark of a complex act of thought equivalent to the simpler act of multipling by the numerator of the fraction; because the other component act, of sub-multipling by positive one, produces no real alteration. Thus, the conceptions of whole numbers, and of reciprocal numbers, are included in the more comprehensive conception of fractional numbers; and a complete theory of the latter would contain all the properties of the former.

17. To form now a notation of fractions, we may agree to denote a fractional number by writing the numerator over the denominator, with a bar between; that is, we may write

$$\mathrm{c} = \frac{\nu}{\mu}\mathrm{b}, \text{ or more fully, } \mathrm{c} = \frac{\nu}{\mu} \times \mathrm{b}, \qquad (121.)$$

when we wish to express that two commensurable steps, b and c, (which we shall, for the present, suppose to be both effective steps,) may be severally formed from some one common base or unit-step a, by multipling that base by the two (positive or contra-positive) whole numbers μ and ν, so that

$$\mathrm{b} = \mu \times \mathrm{a}, \quad \mathrm{c} = \nu \times \mathrm{a}. \qquad (122.)$$

[We shall suppose throughout the whole of this and of the two next following articles, that all the steps are effective, and that all the numerators and denominators are positive or contra-positive, excluding for the present the consideration of null steps, and of null numerators or null denominators.]

Under these conditions, the step c is a fraction of b, and bears to that step b the fractional ratio $\frac{\nu}{\mu}$, called also "the ratio of ν to μ;" and c may be deduced or generated as a product from b by a corresponding act of fractioning, namely, by the act of multiplying b as a multiplicand by the fractional number $\frac{\nu}{\mu}$ as a multiplier, or finally by the complex act of first submultipling b by the denominator μ, and then multipling the result a by the numerator ν. Under the same conditions, it is evident that we may return from c to b by an inverse or reciprocal act of fractioning, namely, by that new complex act which is composed of submultipling instead of multipling by ν, and then multipling instead of submultipling by μ; so that

$$\mathrm{b} = \frac{\mu}{\nu} \times \mathrm{c}, \text{ when } \mathrm{c} = \frac{\nu}{\mu} \times \mathrm{b}: \qquad (123.)$$

on which account we may write

$$\mathrm{b} = \frac{\mu}{\nu} \times \left(\frac{\nu}{\mu} \times \mathrm{b}\right), \text{ and } \mathrm{c} = \frac{\nu}{\mu} \times \left(\frac{\mu}{\nu} \times \mathrm{c}\right), \qquad (124.)$$

whatever (effective) steps may be denoted by b and c, and whatever (positive or contra-positive) whole numbers may be denoted by μ and ν. The two acts of fractioning, marked by the two fractional numbers $\frac{\nu}{\mu}$ and $\frac{\mu}{\nu}$, are therefore opposite or *reciprocal acts*, of which each destroys or undoes the effect of the other; and the fractional numbers themselves may be called *reciprocal fractional numbers*, or, for shortness, *reciprocal fractions:* to mark which reciprocity we may use a new symbol ꓤ, (namely, the initial letter of the word Reciprocatio, distinguished from the other uses of the same letter by being written in an inverted position,) that is, we may write

$$\frac{\nu}{\mu} = \text{ꓤ}\,\frac{\mu}{\nu}, \quad \frac{\mu}{\nu} = \text{ꓤ}\,\frac{\nu}{\mu}, \qquad (125.)$$

whatever positive or contra-positive whole numbers may be marked by μ and ν. In this notation,

$$\text{ꓤ}\,\text{ꓤ}\,\frac{\nu}{\mu} = \text{ꓤ}\left(\text{ꓤ}\,\frac{\nu}{\mu}\right) = \text{ꓤ}\,\frac{\mu}{\nu} = \frac{\nu}{\mu}; \qquad (126.)$$

or, to express the same thing in words, the reciprocal of the reciprocal of any fractional number is that fractional number itself. (Compare equation (57.)).

It is evident also, that

$$\mathrm{a} = \frac{1}{\mu} \times \mathrm{b}, \text{ and } \mathrm{b} = \frac{\mu}{1} \times \mathrm{a}, \text{ if } \mathrm{b} = \mu \times \mathrm{a}; \qquad (127.)$$

that is, the whole number μ, regarded as a multiplier, or as a ratio, may be put under the fractional form $\frac{\mu}{1}$, so that we may write

$$\frac{\mu}{1} = \mu; \qquad (128.)$$

and the reciprocal of this whole number, or the connected reciprocal number $\text{ꓤ}\,\mu$ to multiply by which is equivalent to submultipling by μ, coincides with the reciprocal fractional number $\frac{1}{\mu}$, so that

$$\frac{1}{\mu} = \text{ꓤ}\,\frac{\mu}{1} = \text{ꓤ}\,\mu: \qquad (129.)$$

results which were indeed anticipated in the remarks made at the close of the foregoing article, respecting the extent of the conception of fractional numbers, as including whole numbers and their reciprocals. As an example of these results, the double of any step a may be denoted by the symbol $\frac{2}{1} \times \mathrm{a}$ as well as by $2 \times \mathrm{a}$, and the half of that step a may be denoted either by the symbol $\frac{1}{2} \times \mathrm{a}$, or by $\text{ꓤ}\,2 \times \mathrm{a}$. The symbol $\text{ꓤ}\,1$ is evidently equivalent to 1, the number positive one being its own reciprocal; and the opposite number, contra-positive one, has the same property, because to reverse the direction of a step is an act which destroys itself by repetition, leaving the last resulting step the same as the original; we have therefore the equations,

$$\text{ꓤ}\,1 = 1, \quad \text{ꓤ}\,\Theta\,1 = \Theta\,1. \qquad (130.)$$

By the definition of a fraction, as a multiple of a submultiple, we may now express it as follows:

$$\frac{\nu}{\mu} \times \mathrm{b} = \nu \times \left(\frac{1}{\mu} \times \mathrm{b}\right) = \nu \times (\text{ꓤ}\,\mu \times \mathrm{b}). \qquad (131.)$$

Besides, under the conditions (122.), we have, by (112.) and (114.), that is, by the principle of the indifference of the order in which any two successive multiplings are performed,

$$\mu \times \mathrm{c} = \mu \times (\nu \times \mathrm{a}) = (\mu \times \nu) \times \mathrm{a} = (\nu \times \mu) \times \mathrm{a} = \nu \times (\mu \times \mathrm{a}) = \nu \times \mathrm{b}; \quad (132.)$$

so that a fractional product $\mathrm{c} = \frac{\nu}{\mu} \times \mathrm{b}$ may be derived from the multiplicand b, by first multipling by the numerator ν and then submultipling by the denominator μ, instead of first submultipling by the latter and afterwards multipling by the former; that is, in any act of fractioning, we may change the order of the two successive and component acts of submultipling and multipling, without altering the final result, and may write

$$\frac{\nu}{\mu} \times \text{b} = \frac{1}{\mu} \times (\nu \times \text{b}) = \text{ꝛ}\mu \times (\nu \times \text{b}). \qquad (133.)$$

In general it may easily be shown, by pursuing a reasoning of the same sort, that in any set of acts of multipling and submultipling, to be performed successively on any one original step, the order of succession of those acts may be altered in any arbitrary manner, without altering the final result. We may therefore compound any proposed set of successive acts of fractioning, by compounding first the several acts of submultipling by the several denominators into the one act of submultipling by the product of those denominators, and then the several acts of multipling by the several numerators into the one act of multipling by the product of those numerators, and finally the two acts thus derived into one last resultant act of fractioning; that is, we have the relations,

$$\left.\begin{aligned} \frac{\nu'}{\mu'} \times \left(\frac{\nu}{\mu} \times \text{b}\right) &= \frac{\nu' \times \nu}{\mu' \times \mu} \times \text{b}, \\ \frac{\nu''}{\mu''} \times \left\{\frac{\nu'}{\mu'} \times \left(\frac{\nu}{\mu} \times \text{b}\right)\right\} &= \frac{\nu'' \times \nu' \times \nu}{\mu'' \times \mu' \times \mu} \times \text{b}, \\ \&\text{c.} \end{aligned}\right\} \qquad (134.)$$

We may also introduce or remove any positive or contra-positive whole number as a factor in both the numerator and the denominator of any fraction, without making any real alteration; that is, the following relation holds good:

$$\frac{\nu}{\mu} = \frac{\omega \times \nu}{\omega \times \mu}, \qquad (135.)$$

whatever positive or contra-positive whole numbers may be denoted by $\mu\,\nu\,\omega$; a theorem which may often enable us to put a proposed fraction under a form more simple in itself, or more convenient for comparison with others. As particular cases of this theorem, corresponding to the case when the common factor ω is contra-positive one, we have

$$\frac{\nu}{\mu} = \frac{\Theta\,\nu}{\Theta\,\mu}, \quad \frac{\Theta\,\nu}{\mu} = \frac{\nu}{\Theta\,\mu}; \qquad (136.)$$

that is, the denominator of any fraction may be changed from contra-positive to positive, or from positive to contra-positive, without making any real change, provided that the numerator is also changed to its own opposite whole number. Two fractional numbers, such as $\frac{\Theta\,\nu}{\mu}$ and $\frac{\nu}{\mu}$, may be said to be *opposites*, (though *not recipro-*

cals), when (though *not* themselves the marks of *opposite acts*), they *generate opposite steps*, such as the steps $\frac{\Theta\nu}{\mu} \times b$ and $\frac{\nu}{\mu} \times b$; and to mark this opposition we may write

$$\frac{\Theta\nu}{\mu} = \Theta\frac{\nu}{\mu}. \qquad (137.)$$

Hence every fractional number, with any positive or contra-positive whole numbers μ and ν for its denominator and numerator, may be put under one or other of the two following forms:

$$\text{Ist. } \frac{n}{m}, \quad \text{or} \quad \text{IInd. } \Theta\frac{n}{m}, \qquad (138.)$$

(m and n denoting positive whole numbers,) according as the proposed whole numbers μ and ν agree or differ in respect of being positive or contra-positive; and in the Ist case we may say that the fractional number itself is *positive*, but in the IInd case that it is *contra-positive:* definitions which agree with and include the former conceptions of positive and contra-positive whole numbers, when we consider these as equivalent to fractional numbers in which the numerator is a multiple of the denominator; and lead us to regard the reciprocal of any positive or contra-positive whole number (and more generally the reciprocal of any positive or contra-positive fractional number) as positive or contra-positive like it; a fractional number being equivalent to the reciprocal of a whole number, when the denominator is a multiple of the numerator. A fraction of a late-making step b is itself a late-making or an early-making step, according as the multiplying fractional number is positive or contra-positive; and as we have agreed to write $b > 0$ when b is a late-making step, so we may now agree to write

$$\frac{\nu}{\mu} > 0, \text{ when } \frac{\nu}{\mu} \times b > 0 \text{ and } b > 0, \qquad (139.)$$

that is, when $\frac{\nu}{\mu}$ is a *positive fractional number*, and to write, on the contrary,

$$\frac{\nu}{\mu} < 0, \text{ when } \frac{\nu}{\mu} \times b < 0 \text{ and } b > 0, \qquad (140.)$$

that is, when $\frac{\nu}{\mu}$ is a *contra-positive fractional number*. More generally, we shall write

$$\frac{\nu'}{\mu'} > \frac{\nu}{\mu}, \text{ if } \frac{\nu'}{\mu'} \times b > \frac{\nu}{\mu} \times b, \; b > 0, \qquad (141.)$$

and

$$\frac{\nu'}{\mu'} < \frac{\nu}{\mu}, \text{ if } \frac{\nu'}{\mu'} \times b < \frac{\nu}{\mu} \times b, \; b > 0; \qquad (142.)$$

and shall enunciate these two cases respectively, by saying that in the first case the fractional number $\frac{\nu'}{\mu'}$ is *on the positive side*, and that in the second case it is *on the contra-positive side*, of the other fractional number $\frac{\nu}{\mu}$; or that in the first case $\frac{\nu'}{\mu'}$ *follows* and that in the second it *precedes* $\frac{\nu}{\mu}$, in the general progression of numbers, from contra-positive to positive: definitions which may easily be shown to be consistent with each other, and which extend to whole numbers and their reciprocals, as included in fractional numbers, and to the number zero itself as compared with any of these. Thus, every positive number is on the positive side of zero and of every contra-positive number; while zero is on the positive side of all contra-positive numbers, but on the contra-positive side of all positive numbers: for example,

$$2 > 0,\ 2 > \ominus 3,\ \ominus 3 < 0,\ \ominus 3 < 2,\ 0 > \ominus 3,\ 0 < 2. \qquad (143.)$$

Of two unequal positive whole numbers, the one which has the greater quotity is on the positive side, but among contra-positive numbers the reverse is the case; for example,

$$3 > 2,\ \ominus 3 < \ominus 2: \qquad (144.)$$

and in general a relation of subsequence or precedence between any two whole or fractional numbers is changed to the opposite relation of precedence or subsequence, by altering those numbers to their opposites, though a relation of equality or coincidence remains unaltered after such a change. Among reciprocals of positive whole numbers, the reciprocal of that which has the lesser quotity is on the positive side of the other, while reciprocals of contra-positive numbers are related by the opposite rule; thus

$$\frac{1}{2} > \frac{1}{3},\ \frac{1}{\ominus 2} < \frac{1}{\ominus 3},\ \text{that is, } \text{ɤ}\, 2 > \text{ɤ}\, 3,\ \text{ɤ} \ominus 2 < \text{ɤ} \ominus 3. \qquad (145.)$$

In general, to determine the ordinal relation of any one fractional number $\frac{\nu'}{\mu'}$ to another $\frac{\nu}{\mu}$, as subsequent, or coincident, or precedent, in the general progression of numbers, it is sufficient to prepare them by the principle (135.) so that their denominators may be equal and positive, and then to compare their numerators; for which reason it is always sufficient to compare the two whole numbers $\mu \times \mu \times \mu' \times \nu'$ and $\mu' \times \mu' \times \mu \times \nu$, and we have

$$\frac{\nu'}{\mu'} \begin{matrix} > \\ = \\ < \end{matrix} \frac{\nu}{\mu},\ \text{according as } \mu \times \mu \times \mu' \times \nu' \begin{matrix} > \\ = \\ < \end{matrix} \mu' \times \mu' \times \mu \times \nu: \qquad (146.)$$

the abridged notation $\begin{matrix} > \\ = \\ < \end{matrix}$ implying the same thing as if we had written more fully

"$>$ or $=$ or $<$." If it had been merely required to prepare two fractional numbers so as to make them have a common denominator, without obliging that denominator to be positive, we might have done so in a simpler manner by the formula (135.), namely by multipling the numerator and denominator of each fraction by the denominator of the other fraction, that is, by employing the following expressions,

$$\frac{\nu'}{\mu'} = \frac{\mu \times \nu'}{\mu \times \mu'}, \quad \frac{\nu}{\mu} = \frac{\nu \times \mu'}{\mu \times \mu'}; \qquad (147.)$$

a process which may be still farther simplified when the original denominators have any whole number (other than positive or contra-positive one) for a common factor, since it is sufficient then to multiple by the factors which are not thus common, that is, to employ the expressions,

$$\frac{\nu'}{\omega \times \mu'} = \frac{\mu \times \nu'}{\omega \times \mu \times \mu'}, \quad \frac{\nu}{\omega \times \mu} = \frac{\nu \times \mu'}{\omega \times \mu \times \mu'}. \qquad (148.)$$

A similar process of preparation applies to more fractions than two.

18. This reduction of different fractional numbers to a common denominator is chiefly useful in combining them by certain operations which may be called *algebraical addition and subtraction of fractions*, (from their analogy to the algebraical addition and subtraction of whole numbers, considered in the 14th article, and to the arithmetical operations of addition and subtraction of quotities,) and which present themselves in considering the composition and decomposition of fractional steps. For if we compound, as successive steps, any two or more fractions $\frac{\nu}{\mu} \times \mathrm{b}$, $\frac{\nu'}{\mu'} \times \mathrm{b}$, &c., of any one effective step b, and generate thereby a new effective step, this resultant step will evidently be itself a fraction of the step b, which we may agree to denote as follows:

$$\left.\begin{array}{r} \left(\frac{\nu'}{\mu'} \times \mathrm{b}\right) + \left(\frac{\nu}{\mu} \times \mathrm{b}\right) = \left(\frac{\nu'}{\mu'} + \frac{\nu}{\mu}\right) \times \mathrm{b}, \\ \left(\frac{\nu''}{\mu''} \times \mathrm{b}\right) + \left(\frac{\nu'}{\mu'} \times \mathrm{b}\right) + \left(\frac{\nu}{\mu} \times \mathrm{b}\right) = \left(\frac{\nu''}{\mu''} + \frac{\nu'}{\mu'} + \frac{\nu}{\mu}\right) \times \mathrm{b}, \quad \text{\&c.}; \end{array}\right\} \qquad (149.)$$

and the resultant fractional number $\frac{\nu'}{\mu'} + \frac{\nu}{\mu}$ or $\frac{\nu''}{\mu''} + \frac{\nu'}{\mu'} + \frac{\nu}{\mu}$ &c. may be called the algebraical *sum* of the proposed fractional numbers $\frac{\nu}{\mu}$, $\frac{\nu'}{\mu'}$, $\frac{\nu''}{\mu''}$, &c. and may be said to be formed by algebraically *adding* them together; definitions which agree with those established in the 14th article, when the fractional numbers reduce themselves to whole numbers. If the denominators of the proposed fractions be the same, it is sufficient to add the numerators, because then the proposed fractional steps are all multiples of one common sub-multiple of the common unit-step b, namely of that sub-multiple which is determined by the common denominator; it is therefore sufficient, in other cases, to prepare the fractions so as to satisfy this condition of having a common denominator, and afterwards to add the numerators so prepared, and to combine their sum as the new or resulting numerator of the resulting fractional sum, with the common denominator of the added fractions as the denominator of the same fractional sum; which may, however, be sometimes simplified by the omission of common factors, according to the principle (135.). Thus

$$\frac{\nu'}{\mu'} + \frac{\nu}{\mu} = \frac{(\nu' \times \mu) + (\mu' \times \nu)}{\mu' \times \mu}, \text{ or more concisely } \frac{\nu'}{\mu'} + \frac{\nu}{\mu} = \frac{\nu'\mu + \mu'\nu}{\mu'\mu}, \text{ \&c.}; \quad (150.)$$

for, as a general rule of algebraic notation, we may omit at pleasure the mark of multiplication between any two simple symbols of factors, (except the arithmetical signs 1, 2, 3, &c.,) without causing any confusion; and when a product thus denoted, by the mere juxta-position of its factors, (without the mark ×,) is to be combined with other symbols in the way of addition, by the mark +, it is not necessary to enclose that symbol of a product in parentheses: although in this Elementary Essay we have often used, and shall often use again, these combining and enclosing marks, for greater clearness and fulness. It is evident that the addition of fractions may be performed in any arbitrary order, because the order of composition of the fractional steps is arbitrary.

The algebraical *subtraction* of one given fractional number $\frac{\nu'}{\mu'}$ from another unequal fractional number $\frac{\nu}{\mu}$, is an operation suggested by the decomposition of a given compound fractional step $\frac{\nu}{\mu} \times b$ into a given component fractional step $\frac{\nu'}{\mu'} \times b$ and a sought component fractional step $\frac{\nu''}{\mu''} \times b$, (these three steps being here supposed to be all effective:) and it may be performed by compounding the opposite of the given component step with the given compound step, or by algebraically adding the opposite $\ominus \frac{\nu'}{\mu'}$ of the given fractional number $\frac{\nu'}{\mu'}$ to the other given fractional number $\frac{\nu}{\mu}$, according to the rule (150.). When we thus subtract one fractional number from another with which it does not coincide, the result is positive or contra-positive according as the fraction from which we subtract is on the positive or contra-positive side of the other; and thus we have another general method, besides the rule (146.), for examining the ordinal relation of any two unequal fractions, in the general progression of numbers. This ordinal relation between any two fractional (or whole) numbers α and β, is not altered by adding any fractional (or whole) number γ to both, nor by subtracting it from both; so that

$$\gamma+\beta \gtreqless \gamma + \alpha, \text{ and } \Theta\,\gamma \dotplus \beta \gtreqless \Theta\,\gamma + \alpha, \text{according as } \beta \gtreqless \alpha. \qquad (151.)$$

19. Again, the composition and decomposition of *successive acts of fractioning* (instead of successive fractional *steps*) conduct to algebraical operations of *multiplication* and *division* of fractional numbers, which are analogous to the arithmetical operations of multiplication and division of quotities. For if we first multiply a given step b by a given fractional number $\frac{\nu}{\mu}$, that is, if we first perform on b the act of fractioning denoted by this number, and so form the fractional step $\frac{\nu}{\mu} \times$ b, we may then perform on the result another act of fractioning denoted by another fractional number $\frac{\nu'}{\mu'}$, and so deduce another fractional step $\frac{\nu'}{\mu'} \times \left(\frac{\nu}{\mu} \times \text{b}\right)$, which will evidently be itself a fraction of the original step b, and might therefore have been deduced from b by one compound act of fractioning; and thus we may proceed to other and other fractions of that step, and to other compound acts of fractioning, which may be thus denoted,

$$\left.\begin{array}{l} \frac{\nu'}{\mu'} \times \left(\frac{\nu}{\mu} \times \text{b}\right) = \left(\frac{\nu'}{\mu'} \times \frac{\nu}{\mu}\right) \times \text{b}, \\ \frac{\nu''}{\mu''} \times \left\{\frac{\nu'}{\mu'} \times \left(\frac{\nu}{\mu} \times \text{b}\right)\right\} = \left(\frac{\nu''}{\mu''} \times \frac{\nu'}{\mu'} \times \frac{\nu}{\mu}\right) \times \text{b}, \quad \&c.; \end{array}\right\} \qquad (152.)$$

and the resultant fractional numbers $\frac{\nu'}{\mu'} \times \frac{\nu}{\mu}$, $\frac{\nu''}{\mu''} \times \frac{\nu'}{\mu'} \times \frac{\nu}{\mu}$, &c., which thus express the resultant acts of fractioning, derived from the proposed component acts marked by the fractional numbers $\frac{\nu}{\mu}$, $\frac{\nu'}{\mu'}$, $\frac{\nu''}{\mu''}$, &c., may be called the *algebraic products* of those proposed fractional numbers, and may be said to be formed by *algebraically multiplying* them as *fractional factors* together; definitions which agree with the definitions of product and multiplication already established for whole numbers. The same definitions shew that every fraction may be regarded as the product of the numerator (as one factor) and the reciprocal of the denominator (as another); and give, in general, by (134.), the following rule for the calculation of a fractional product

$$\frac{\nu'}{\mu'} \times \frac{\nu}{\mu} = \frac{\nu' \times \nu}{\mu' \times \mu}, \quad \frac{\nu''}{\mu''} \times \frac{\nu'}{\mu'} \times \frac{\nu}{\mu} = \frac{\nu'' \times \nu' \times \nu}{\mu'' \times \mu' \times \mu}, \ \&c. \qquad (153.)$$

The properties (114.) and (115.) of algebraic products of whole numbers extend to products of fractional numbers also; that is, we may change in any manner the order of the fractional factors; and if we resolve any one of those factors into two or more algebraic parts by the rules of algebraic addition and subtraction, we may combine each part separately as a partial factor with the other factors proposed, so as to form by algebraic multiplication a partial fractional product, and then add together those partial products algebraically to obtain the total product: or, in written symbols,

$$\frac{\nu'}{\mu'} \times \frac{\nu}{\mu} = \frac{\nu}{\mu} \times \frac{\nu'}{\mu'}, \text{ \&c.,} \qquad (154.)$$

and

$$\frac{\nu}{\mu} \times \left(\frac{\nu''}{\mu''} + \frac{\nu'}{\mu'}\right) = \left(\frac{\nu}{\mu} \times \frac{\nu''}{\mu''}\right) + \left(\frac{\nu}{\mu} \times \frac{\nu'}{\mu'}\right), \text{ \&c.,} \qquad (155.)$$

because

$$\frac{\nu}{\mu} \times \left(\mathfrak{b}'' + \mathfrak{b}'\right) = \left(\frac{\nu}{\mu} \times \mathfrak{b}''\right) + \left(\frac{\nu}{\mu} \times \mathfrak{b}'\right), \qquad (156.)$$

whatever steps may be denoted by $\mathfrak{b}'$ and $\mathfrak{b}''$ and whatever fractional (or whole) number by $\frac{\nu}{\mu}$. We may also remark that

$$\gamma \times \beta \gtreqless \gamma \times \alpha, \text{ according as } \beta \gtreqless \alpha, \text{ if } \gamma > 0, \qquad (157.)$$

but that

$$\gamma \times \beta \lesseqgtr \gamma \times \alpha, \text{ according as } \beta \gtreqless \alpha, \text{ if } \gamma < 0, \qquad (158.)$$

$\alpha\ \beta\ \gamma$ denoting any three fractional (or whole) numbers.

The deduction of one of two fractional factors from the other and from the product, may be called (by analogy to arithmetic) the *algebraic division* of the given fractional product as a *dividend*, by the given fractional factor as a *divisor;* and the result, which may be called the *quotient*, may always be found by algebraically multiplying the proposed dividend by the reciprocal of the proposed divisor. This more general conception of quotient, agrees with the process of the 15th article, for the division of one whole number by another, when that process gives an accurate quotient in whole numbers; and when no such integral and accurate quotient can be found, we may still, by our present extended definitions, conceive the numerator of any fraction to be divided by the denominator, and the quotient of this division will be the fractional number itself. In this last case, the fractional number is not exactly equal to any whole number, but lies between two successive whole numbers, a next preceding and a next succeeding, in the general progression of numbers; and these may be discovered by the process of approximate division above mentioned, while each of the two remainders of that approximate division is the numerator of a new fraction, which retains the proposed denominator, and must be added algebraically as a *correction* to the corresponding *approximate integer quotient*, in order to express, by the help of it, the quotient of the accurate division. For example,

$$\frac{8}{5} = \frac{3}{5} + 1 = \frac{\Theta\, 2}{5} + 2, \text{ and } \frac{\Theta\, 8}{5} = \frac{2}{5} + \Theta\, 2 = \frac{\Theta\, 3}{5} + \Theta\, 1.$$

In general, a fractional number may be called a *mixed number*, when it is thus expressed as the algebraic sum of a whole number and a *proper fraction*, this last name being given to a fractional number which lies between zero and positive or contra-positive one. We may remark that an ordinal relation between two fractional numbers is not altered by dividing them both by one common positive divisor; but if the divisor be contra-positive, it changes a relation of subsequence to one of precedence, and conversely, without disturbing a relation of coincidence.

20. In all the formulæ of the three last articles, we have supposed that all the numerators and all the denominators of those formulæ are positive or contra-positive whole numbers, excluding the number zero. However, the general conception of a fraction as *a multiple of a sub-multiple*, permits us to suppose that the multipling number or numerator is zero, and shows us that then the fractional step itself is null, if the denominator be different from zero; that is,

$$\frac{0}{\mu} \times \mathrm{b} = 0 \text{ if } \mu \neq 0. \qquad (159.)$$

Thus, although we supposed, in the composition (149.) of successive fractional steps, (with positive or contra-positive numerators and denominators,) that the resultant step was effective, yet we might have removed this limitation, and have presented the formulæ (150.) for fractional sums as extending even to the case when the resultant step is null, if we had observed that in every such case the resultant numerator of the formula is zero, while the resultant denominator is different from zero, and therefore that the formula rightly expresses that the resultant fraction or sum is null. For example, the addition of any two opposite fractional numbers, such as $\frac{\nu}{\mu}$ and $\frac{\Theta\,\nu}{\mu}$, in which μ and ν are different from zero, conducts to a null sum, under the form $\frac{\Theta\,\nu+\nu}{\mu}$, in which the numerator $\Theta\,\nu+\nu$ is zero, while the denominator is different from zero.

But it is not so immediately clear what ought to be regarded as the meaning of a fractional sign, in the case when the denominator is null, and when therefore the act of fractioning prescribed by the notation involves a sub-multipling by zero. To discuss this case, we must remember that to sub-multiple a step b by a whole number μ, is, by its definition, to find another step a, which, when multipled by that whole number μ, shall produce the proposed step b; but, whatever step a may be, the theory of multiple steps (explained in the 13th article) shows that it necessarily produces the null step 0, when it is multipled by the null number zero; that is, the equation

$$0 \times a = 0 \qquad (160.)$$

is true independently of a, and consequently we have always

$$0 \times a \neq b, \text{ if } b \neq 0. \qquad (161.)$$

It is, therefore, impossible to find any step a, in the whole progression of time, which shall satisfy the equation

$$\frac{1}{0} \times b = a, \text{ or } 0 \times a = b, \qquad (162.)$$

if the given step b be effective; or, in other words, it is impossible to sub-multiple an effective step by zero. The fractional sign $\frac{1}{0}$ denotes therefore an *impossible act,* if it be applied to an effective step: and *the zero-submultiple of an effective step* is a phrase which involves a contradiction. On the other hand, if the given step b be null, it is not only possible to choose some one step a which shall satisfy the equations (162.), but every conceivable step possesses the same proposed property; in this case, therefore, the proposed conditions lay no restriction on the result, but at the same time, and for the same reason, they fail to give any information respecting it: and the act of sub-multipling a null step by zero, is indeed a possible, but it is also an *indeterminate act,* or an act with an indeterminate result; so that the *zero-submultiple of a null step,* and the written symbol $\frac{1}{0} \times 0$, are spoken or written signs which do not specify any thing, although they do not involve a contradiction. We see then that while a fractional number is in general the sign of a possible and determinate act of fractioning, it loses one or other of those two essential characters whenever its denominator is zero; for which reason it becomes comparatively unfit, or at least inconvenient, in this case, for the purposes of mathematical reasoning. And to prevent the confusion which might arise from the mixture of such cases with others, it is convenient to lay down this *general rule,* to which we shall henceforth adhere: that *all denominators and divisors are to be supposed different from zero* unless the contrary be mentioned expressly; or that we shall *never sub-multiple nor divide by a null number* without expressly recording that we do so.

On the Comparison of any one effective Step with any other, in the way of Ratio, and the Generation of any one such step from any other, in the way of Multiplication; and on the Addition, Subtraction, Multiplication, and Division of Algebraic Numbers in general, considered thus as Ratios or as Multipliers of Steps.

21. The foregoing remarks upon fractions lead naturally to the more general conception of *algebraic ratio*, as a complex relation of any one effective step to any other, determined by their *relative largeness* and *relative direction*; and to a similarly extended conception of algebraic *multiplication*, as an *act* (of thought) which enlarges, or preserves, or diminishes the magnitude, while it preserves or reverses the direction, of any effective step proposed. In conformity with these conceptions, and by analogy to our former notations, if we denote by a and b any two effective steps, of which a may be called the *antecedent* or the *multiplicand*, and b the *consequent* or the *product*, we may employ the symbol $\frac{\mathrm{b}}{\mathrm{a}}$ to denote the *ratio* of the consequent b to the antecedent a, or the algebraic *number* or *multiplier* by which we are to multiply a as a *multiplicand* in order to generate b as a product: and if we still employ the mark of multiplication $\times$, we may now write, in general,

$$\mathrm{b} = \frac{\mathrm{b}}{\mathrm{a}} \times \mathrm{a}: \qquad (163.)$$

or, more concisely,

$$\mathrm{b} = a \times \mathrm{a}, \text{ if } \frac{\mathrm{b}}{\mathrm{a}} = a, \qquad (164.)$$

that is, if we employ, for abridgement, a simple symbol, such as the italic letter a, to denote the same ratio or multiplier which is more fully denoted by the complex symbol $\frac{\mathrm{b}}{\mathrm{a}}$.

It is an immediate consequence of these conceptions and definitions, that the following relation holds good,

$$\frac{\nu \times \mathrm{a}}{\mu \times \mathrm{a}} = \frac{\nu}{\mu}, \qquad (165.)$$

a denoting any effective step, and μ and ν denoting any positive or contra-positive whole numbers; since the fractional ratio denoted by the symbol $\frac{\nu}{\mu}$ is the ratio of the multiple step $\nu \times a$ to the multiple step $\mu \times a$. In like manner it follows, from the same conceptions and definitions, that

$$\frac{\frac{\nu}{\mu} \times b}{b} = \frac{\nu}{\mu}, \text{ and reciprocally } b' = \frac{\nu}{\mu} \times b \text{ if } \frac{b'}{b} = \frac{\nu}{\mu}; \qquad (166.)$$

and more generally, that

$$\frac{\frac{b}{a} \times c}{c} = \frac{b}{a}, \qquad (167.)$$

and reciprocally,

$$d = \frac{b}{a} \times c \text{ if } \frac{d}{c} = \frac{b}{a}; \qquad (168.)$$

whatever effective steps may be denoted by a, b, c, d, and whatever fraction by $\frac{\nu}{\mu}$.

We may also conceive combinations of ratios with each other, by operations which we may call Addition, Subtraction, Multiplication, and Division of Ratios, or of *general algebraic numbers*, from the analogy of these operations to those which we have already called by the same names, in the theories of whole numbers and of fractions. And as we wrote, in treating of whole numbers,

$$\omega = \nu + \mu \text{ when } \omega \times a = (\nu \times a) + (\mu \times a), \qquad (107.)$$

and

$$\omega = \nu \times \mu \text{ when } \omega \times a = \nu \times (\mu \times a); \qquad (111.)$$

and, in the theory of fractions,

$$\frac{\nu''}{\mu''} = \frac{\nu'}{\mu'} + \frac{\nu}{\mu} \text{ when } \frac{\nu''}{\mu''} \times b = \left(\frac{\nu'}{\mu'} \times b\right) + \left(\frac{\nu}{\mu} \times b\right), \qquad (149.)$$

and

$$\frac{\nu''}{\mu''} = \frac{\nu'}{\mu'} \times \frac{\nu}{\mu} \text{ when } \frac{\nu''}{\mu''} \times b = \frac{\nu'}{\mu'} \times \left(\frac{\nu}{\mu} \times b\right), \qquad (152.)$$

with other similar expressions; so we shall now write, in the more general theory of ratios,

$$\frac{b''}{a''} = \frac{b'}{a'} + \frac{b}{a} \text{ when } \frac{b''}{a''} \times c = \left(\frac{b'}{a'} \times c\right) + \left(\frac{b}{a} \times c\right), \qquad (169.)$$

and

$$\frac{b''}{a''} = \frac{b'}{a'} \times \frac{b}{a}, \text{ when } \frac{b''}{a''} \times c = \frac{b'}{a'} \times \left(\frac{b}{a} \times c\right): \qquad (170.)$$

and shall suppose that similar definitions are established for the algebraical sums and products of more than two ratios, or general algebraic numbers. It follows that

$$\left.\begin{array}{c} \dfrac{b'}{a}+\dfrac{b}{a}=\dfrac{b'+b}{a} \\ \dfrac{b''}{a}+\dfrac{b'}{a}+\dfrac{b}{a}=\dfrac{b''+b'+b}{a}, \\ \&c. \end{array}\right\} \qquad (171.)$$

and that

$$\left.\begin{array}{c} \dfrac{b'}{b}\times\dfrac{b}{a}=\dfrac{b'}{a}, \\ \dfrac{b''}{b'}\times\dfrac{b'}{b}\times\dfrac{b}{a}=\dfrac{b''}{a}, \quad \&c. \end{array}\right\} \qquad (172.)$$

A ratio between any two effective steps may be said to be *positive* or *contra-positive*, according as those two steps are *co-directional* or *contra-directional*, that is, according as their directions agree or differ; and then the product of any two or more positive or contra-positive ratios will evidently be contra-positive or positive according as there are or are not an odd number of contra-positive ratios, as factors of this product; because the direction of a step is not altered or is restored, if it either be not reversed at all, or be reversed an even number of times.

Again, we may say, as in the case of fractions, that we *subtract* a ratio when we add its *opposite*, and that we *divide* by a ratio when we multiply by its *reciprocal*, if we agree to say that two ratios or numbers are *opposites* when they generate *opposite steps* by multiplication from one common step as a multiplicand, and if we call them *reciprocals* when their corresponding acts of multiplication are *opposite acts*, which destroy, each, the effect of the other; and we may mark such opposites and reciprocals, by writing, as in the notation of fractions,

$$\frac{b'}{a'}=\Theta\,\frac{b}{a} \text{ when } \frac{b'}{a'}\times c=\Theta\left(\frac{b}{a}\times c\right), \qquad (173.)$$

and

$$\frac{b'}{a'}=\text{Я}\,\frac{b}{a}, \text{ when } \frac{b'}{a'}\times\left(\frac{b}{a}\times c\right)=c: \qquad (174.)$$

definitions from which it follows that

$$\frac{\Theta\, b}{a}=\Theta\,\frac{b}{a}, \qquad (175.)$$

and that

$$\frac{a}{b}=\text{Я}\,\frac{b}{a}. \qquad (176.)$$

And as, by our conceptions and notations respecting the ordinal relation of one fractional number to another, (as subsequent, or coincident, or precedent, in the general progression of such numbers from contra-positive to positive,) we had the relations,

$$\frac{\nu'}{\mu'} \overset{>}{\underset{<}{=}} \frac{\nu}{\mu}, \text{ when } \frac{\nu'}{\mu'} \times \mathrm{a} \overset{>}{\underset{<}{=}} \frac{\nu}{\mu} \times \mathrm{a}, \quad \mathrm{a} > 0;$$

so we may now establish, by analogous conceptions and notations respecting ratios, the relations,

$$\frac{\mathrm{b}''}{\mathrm{a}''} \overset{>}{\underset{<}{=}} \frac{\mathrm{b}'}{\mathrm{a}'}, \text{ when } \frac{\mathrm{b}''}{\mathrm{a}''} \times \mathrm{a} \overset{>}{\underset{<}{=}} \frac{\mathrm{b}'}{\mathrm{a}'} \times \mathrm{a}, \quad \mathrm{a} > 0: \qquad (177.)$$

that is, more fully,

$$\frac{\mathrm{b}''}{\mathrm{a}''} > \frac{\mathrm{b}}{\mathrm{a}}, \text{ when } \left(\frac{\mathrm{b}''}{\mathrm{a}''} \times \mathrm{a}\right) + \mathrm{A} > \left(\frac{\mathrm{b}'}{\mathrm{a}'} \times \mathrm{a}\right) + \mathrm{A}, \qquad (178.)$$

$$\frac{\mathrm{b}''}{\mathrm{a}''} = \frac{\mathrm{b}'}{\mathrm{a}'}, \text{ when } \left(\frac{\mathrm{b}''}{\mathrm{a}''} \times \mathrm{a}\right) + \mathrm{A} = \left(\frac{\mathrm{b}'}{\mathrm{a}'} \times \mathrm{a}\right) + \mathrm{A}, \qquad (179.)$$

and

$$\frac{\mathrm{b}''}{\mathrm{a}''} < \frac{\mathrm{b}'}{\mathrm{a}'}, \text{ when } \left(\frac{\mathrm{b}''}{\mathrm{a}''} \times \mathrm{a}\right) + \mathrm{A} < \left(\frac{\mathrm{b}'}{\mathrm{a}'} \times \mathrm{a}\right) + \mathrm{A}; \qquad (180.)$$

the symbol A denoting any moment of time, and a any late-making step. The relation (179.) is indeed an immediate consequence of the first conceptions of steps and ratios; but it is inserted here along with the relations (178.) and (180.), to show more distinctly in what manner the comparison and arrangement of the moments

$$\left(\frac{\mathrm{b}'}{\mathrm{a}'} \times \mathrm{a}\right) + \mathrm{A}, \left(\frac{\mathrm{b}''}{\mathrm{a}''} \times \mathrm{a}\right) + \mathrm{A}, \text{ \&c.} \qquad (181.)$$

which are suggested and determined by the ratios or numbers $\frac{\mathrm{b}'}{\mathrm{a}'}$, $\frac{\mathrm{b}''}{\mathrm{a}''}$, &c., (in combination with a standard moment A and with a late-making step a,) enable us to compare and arrange those ratios or numbers themselves, and to conceive an indefinite progression of ratio from contra-positive to positive, including the indefinite progression of whole numbers (103.), and the more comprehensive progression of fractional numbers considered in the 17th article: for it will soon be shown, that though every fractional number is a ratio, yet there are many ratios which cannot be expressed under the form of fractional numbers. Meanwhile we may observe, that the theorems (151.) (157.) (158.) respecting the ordinal relations of fractions in the general progression of number, are true, even when the symbols α β γ denote ratios which are not reducible to the fractional form; and that this indefinite progression

of number, or of ratio, from contra-positive to positive, corresponds in all respects to the thought from which it was deduced, of the progression of time itself, from moments indefinitely early to moments indefinitely late.

22. It is manifest, on a little attention, that the ratio of one effective step b to another a, is a relation which is entirely determined when those steps are given, but which is not altered by multiplying both those steps by any common multiplier, whether positive or contra-positive; for the *relative largeness* of the two steps is not altered by doubling or halving both, or by enlarging or diminishing the magnitudes of both in any other common ratio of magnitude, that is, by multiplying both by any common positive multiplier: nor is their *relative direction* altered, by reversing the directions of both. We have then, generally,

$$\frac{\frac{b'}{a'} \times b}{\frac{b'}{a'} \times a} = \frac{b}{a}; \qquad (182.)$$

and in particular, by changing a′ to a, and b′ to c,

$$\frac{\frac{c}{a} \times b}{c} = \frac{b}{a}. \qquad (183.)$$

Hence, by (167.), the two steps $\frac{c}{a} \times b$ and $\frac{b}{a} \times c$ are related in one common ratio, namely the ratio $\frac{b}{a}$, to the common step c, and therefore are equivalent to each other; that is, we have the equation,

$$\frac{c}{a} \times b = \frac{b}{a} \times c, \qquad (184.)$$

whatever three effective steps may be denoted by a b c.

In general, when any four effective steps a b c d are connected by the relation

$$\frac{d}{c} = \frac{b}{a}, \qquad (185.)$$

that is, when the ratio of the step d to c is the same as the ratio of the step b to a, these two pairs of steps a, b and c, d may be said to be *analogous* or *proportional pairs*; the steps a and c being called the *antecedents* of the analogy, (or of the proportion) and the steps b and d being called the *consequents*, while a and d are the *extremes* and b and c the *means*. And since the last of these four steps, or the second consequent d, may, by (168.), be expressed by the symbol $\frac{b}{a} \times c$, we see, by (184.), that it bears to the first consequent b the ratio $\frac{c}{a}$ of the second antecedent c to the first antecedent a; that is,

$$\frac{\mathrm{d}}{\mathrm{b}} = \frac{\mathrm{c}}{\mathrm{a}} \text{ if } \frac{\mathrm{d}}{\mathrm{c}} = \frac{\mathrm{b}}{\mathrm{a}}: \qquad (186.)$$

a theorem which shows that we may transform the expression of an *analogy* (or *proportion*) between two pairs of effective steps in a manner which may be called *alternation.* (Compare the theorem (11.).)

It is still more easy to perceive that we may *invert* an analogy or proportion between any two pairs of effective steps; or that the following theorem is true,

$$\frac{\mathrm{c}}{\mathrm{d}} = \frac{\mathrm{a}}{\mathrm{b}}, \text{ if } \frac{\mathrm{d}}{\mathrm{c}} = \frac{\mathrm{b}}{\mathrm{a}}. \qquad (187.)$$

Combining inversion with alternation, we see that

$$\frac{\mathrm{b}}{\mathrm{d}} = \frac{\mathrm{a}}{\mathrm{c}}, \text{ if } \frac{\mathrm{d}}{\mathrm{c}} = \frac{\mathrm{b}}{\mathrm{a}}. \qquad (188.)$$

(Compare the theorems (12.) and (13.).)

In general, if any two pairs of effective steps a, b and c, d be analogous, we do not disturb this analogy by interchanging the extremes among themselves, or the means among themselves, or by substituting extremes for means and means for extremes; or by altering *proportionally,* that is, altering in one common ratio, or multiplying by one common multiplier, whether positive or contra-positive, the two consequents, or the two antecedents, or the two steps of either pair: or, finally, by altering *in inverse proportion,* that is, multiplying respectively by any two reciprocal multipliers, the two extremes, or the two means. The analogy (185.) may therefore be expressed, not only in the ways (186.), (187.), (188.), but also in the following:

$$\frac{a \times \mathrm{d}}{\mathrm{c}} = \frac{a \times \mathrm{b}}{\mathrm{a}}, \quad \frac{\mathrm{d}}{a \times \mathrm{c}} = \frac{\mathrm{b}}{a \times \mathrm{a}}, \quad \frac{a \times \mathrm{d}}{a \times \mathrm{c}} = \frac{\mathrm{b}}{\mathrm{a}}, \qquad (189.)$$

$$\frac{\text{ᴚ}\, a \times \mathrm{d}}{\mathrm{c}} = \frac{\mathrm{b}}{a \times \mathrm{a}}, \quad \frac{\mathrm{d}}{\text{ᴚ}\, a \times \mathrm{c}} = \frac{a \times \mathrm{b}}{\mathrm{a}}, \qquad (190.)$$

a denoting any ratio of one effective step to another, and $\text{ᴚ}\, a$ denoting the reciprocal ratio, of the latter step to the former.

23. We may also consider it as evident that if any effective step c be compounded of any others a and b, this relation of compound and components will not be disturbed by altering the magnitudes of all in any common ratio of magnitude, that is by doubling or halving it, or multiplying all by any common positive multiplier; and we saw, in the 12th article, that the same relation of compound and components is not disturbed by reversing the directions of all: we may therefore mul-

tiply all by any common multiplier a, whether positive or contra-positive, and may establish the theorem,

$$a \times \mathrm{c} = (a \times \mathrm{b}) + (a \times \mathrm{a}), \text{ if } \mathrm{c} = \mathrm{b} + \mathrm{a}; \qquad (191.)$$

which gives, by the definitions (169.) (170.) for the sum and product of two ratios, this other important relation,

$$a \times (b' + b) = (a \times b') + (a \times b), \qquad (192.)$$

if b, b', and $b' + b$, denote any three positive or contra-positive numbers, connected with each other by the definition (169.), or by the following condition,

$$(b' + b) \times \mathrm{a} = (b' \times \mathrm{a}) + (b \times \mathrm{a}), \qquad (193.)$$

in which a denotes any arbitrary effective step. The definitions of the sum and product of two ratios, or algebraic numbers, give still more simply the theorem,

$$(b' + b) \times a = (b' \times a) + (b \times a). \qquad (194.)$$

The definition (169.) of a sum of two ratios, when combined with the theorem (75.) respecting the arbitrary order of composition of two successive steps, gives the following similar theorem respecting the addition of two ratios,

$$b + a = a + b. \qquad (195.)$$

And if the definition (170.) of a product of two ratios or multipliers be combined with the theorem (186.) of alternation of an analogy between two pairs of steps, in the same way as the definition of a compound step was combined in the 12th article with the theorem of alternation of an analogy between two pairs of moments, it shows that as any two steps a, b, may be applied to any moment, or compounded with each other, either in one or in the opposite order, ($\mathrm{b} + \mathrm{a} = \mathrm{a} + \mathrm{b}$,) so any two ratios a and b may be applied as multipliers to any step, or combined as factors of a product with each other, in an equally arbitrary order; that is, we have the relation,

$$b \times a = a \times b. \qquad (196.)$$

It is easy to infer, from the theorems (195.) (196.), that the opposite of a sum of two ratios is the sum of the opposites of those ratios, and that the reciprocal of the product of two ratios is the product of their two reciprocals; that is,

$$\Theta\,(b + a) = \Theta\, b + \Theta\, a, \qquad (197.)$$

and

$$\text{ᴙ}\,(b \times a) = \text{ᴙ}\, b \times \text{ᴙ}\, a. \qquad (198.)$$

And all the theorems of this article, respecting pairs of ratios or of steps, may easily be extended to the comparison and combination of more ratios or steps than two. In particular, when any number of ratios are to be added or multiplied together, we may arrange them in any arbitrary order; and in any multiplication of ratios, we may treat any one factor as the algebraic sum of any number of other ratios, or partial factors, and substitute each of these separately and successively for it, and the sum of the partial products thus obtained will be the total product sought. As an example of the multiplication of ratios, considered thus as sums, it is plain from the foregoing principles that

$$(d+c)\times(b+a)=\{d\times(b+a)\}+\{c\times(b+a)\}$$
$$=(d\times b)+(d\times a)+(c\times b)+(c\times a)$$
$$=d\,b+d\,a+c\,b+c\,a, \qquad (199.)$$

and that

$$(b+a)\times(b+a)=(b\times b)+(2\times b\times a)+(a\times a)$$
$$=b\,b+2\,b\,a+a\,a, \qquad (200.)$$

whatever positive or contra-positive ratios may be denoted by $a\ b\ c\ d$.

And though we have only considered effective steps, and positive or contra-positive ratios, (or algebraic numbers,) in the few last articles of this Essay, yet the results extend to null steps, and to null ratios, also; provided that for the reasons given in the 20th article we treat all such null steps as consequents only and not as antecedents of ratios, admitting null ratios themselves but not their reciprocals into our formulæ, or employing null numbers as multipliers only but not as divisors, in order to avoid the introduction of symbols which suggest either impossible or indeterminate operations.

On the insertion of a Mean Proportional between two steps; and on Impossible, Ambiguous, and Incommensurable Square-Roots of Ratios.

24. Three effective steps $\mathrm{a}\ \mathrm{b}\ \mathrm{b}'$ may be said to form a *continued analogy* or *continued proportion*, when the ratio of b' to b is the same as that of b to a, that is, when

$$\frac{\mathrm{b}'}{\mathrm{b}}=\frac{\mathrm{b}}{\mathrm{a}}; \qquad (201.)$$

a and b′ being then the *extremes*, and b the *mean*, or the *mean proportional* between a and b′, in this continued analogy; in which b′ is also the *third proportional* to a and b, and a is at the same time the third proportional to b′ and b, because the analogy may be inverted thus,

$$\frac{\mathrm{a}}{\mathrm{b}} = \frac{\mathrm{b}}{\mathrm{b}'}. \qquad (202.)$$

When the condition (201.) is satisfied, we may express b′ as follows,

$$\mathrm{b}' = \frac{\mathrm{b}}{\mathrm{a}} \times \mathrm{a}; \qquad (203.)$$

that is, if we denote by a the ratio of b to a, we shall have the relations

$$\mathrm{b} = a \times \mathrm{a}, \ \mathrm{b}' = a \times \mathrm{b} = a \times a \times \mathrm{a}; \qquad (204.)$$

and reciprocally when these relations exist, we can conclude the existence of the continued analogy (201.). It is clear that whatever effective steps may be denoted by a and b, we can always determine, (or conceive determined,) in this manner, one third proportional b′ and only one; that is, we can complete the continued analogy (201.) in one, but in only one way, when an extreme a and the mean b are given: and it is important to observe that whether the ratio a of the given mean b to the given extreme a be positive or contra-positive, that is, whether the two given steps a and b be co-directional or contra-directional steps, the product $a \times a$ will necessarily be a positive ratio, and therefore the deduced extreme step b′ will necessarily be co-directional with the given extreme step a. In fact, without recurring to the theorem of the 21st article respecting the cases in which a product of contra-positive factors is positive, it is plain that the continued analogy requires, by its conception, that the step b′ should be co-directional to b, if b be co-directional to a, and that b′ should be contra-directional to b if b be contra-directional to a; so that in every possible case the extremes themselves are co-directional, as both agreeing with the mean or both differing from the mean in direction. *It is, therefore, impossible to insert a mean proportional between two contra-directional steps;* but for the same reason *we may insert either of two opposite steps as a mean proportional between two given co-directional steps;* namely, either a step which agrees with each, or a step which differs from each in direction, while the common magnitude of these two opposite steps is exactly intermediate in the way of ratio between the magnitudes of the two given extremes. (We here assume, as it seems reasonable to do, the conception of the general existence of such an exactly intermediate magnitude, although the nature and necessity of this conception will soon be more fully considered.) For example, it is impossible to insert a mean proportional between the two contra-directional (effective) steps a and $\Theta\, 9$ a, that is, it is impossible to find any step b which shall satisfy the conditions of the continued analogy

$$\frac{\Theta\, 9\, \mathrm{a}}{\mathrm{b}} = \frac{\mathrm{b}}{\mathrm{a}}, \qquad (205.)$$

or any number or ratio a which shall satisfy the equation

$$a \times a = \Theta\, 9: \qquad (206.)$$

whereas it is possible to insert in two different ways a mean proportional b between the two co-directional (effective) steps a and 9 a, or to satisfy by two different steps b (namely, by the step 3 a, and also by the opposite step $\Theta\, 3$ a) the conditions of the continued analogy

$$\frac{9\, \mathrm{a}}{\mathrm{b}} = \frac{\mathrm{b}}{\mathrm{a}}, \qquad (207.)$$

and it is possible to satisfy by two different ratios a the equation

$$a \times a = 9, \qquad (208.)$$

namely, either by the ratio 3 or by the opposite ratio $\Theta\, 3$. In general, we may agree to express the two opposite ratios a which satisfy the equation

$$a \times a = b \ (> 0), \qquad (209.)$$

by the two symbols

$$\sqrt{b} \ (> 0) \text{ and } \Theta \sqrt{b} \ (< 0), \qquad (210.)$$

b and $\sqrt{b}$ being positive ratios, but $\Theta \sqrt{b}$ being contra-positive; for example,

$$\sqrt{9} = 3, \quad \Theta \sqrt{9} = \Theta\, 3. \qquad (211.)$$

With this notation we may represent the two opposite steps of which each is a mean proportional between two given co-directional (effective) steps a and b′, by the symbols

$$\sqrt{\frac{\mathrm{b}'}{\mathrm{a}}} \times \mathrm{a}, \text{ and } \Theta \sqrt{\frac{\mathrm{b}'}{\mathrm{a}}} \times \mathrm{a}; \qquad (212.)$$

and shall have for each the equation of a continued analogy,

$$\frac{\mathrm{b}'}{\sqrt{\frac{\mathrm{b}'}{\mathrm{a}}} \times \mathrm{a}} = \frac{\sqrt{\frac{\mathrm{b}'}{\mathrm{a}}} \times \mathrm{a}}{\mathrm{a}}, \quad \frac{\mathrm{b}'}{\Theta \sqrt{\frac{\mathrm{b}'}{\mathrm{a}}} \times \mathrm{a}} = \frac{\Theta \sqrt{\frac{\mathrm{b}'}{\mathrm{a}}} \times \mathrm{a}}{\mathrm{a}}. \qquad (213.)$$

We may also call the numbers $\sqrt{b}$ and $\ominus \sqrt{b}$ by the common name of *roots*, or (more fully) *square-roots* of the positive number b; distinguishing them from each other by the separate names of the *positive square-root* and the *contra-positive square-root* of that number b, which may be called their common *square*: though we may sometimes speak simply of *the square-root* of a (positive) number, meaning then the positive root, which is simpler and more important than the other.

25. The idea of the *continuity of the progression from moment to moment in time* involves the idea of a similarly *continuous progression in magnitude* from any one effective step or interval between two different moments, to any other unequal effective step or other unequal interval; and also the idea of a *continuous progression in ratio*, from any one degree of inequality, in the way of relative largeness or smallness, as a relation between two steps, to any other degree. Pursuing this train of thought, we find ourselves compelled to conceive the existence (assumed in the last article) of a determined magnitude b, exactly intermediate in the way of ratio between any two given unequal magnitudes a and b′, that is, larger or smaller than the one, in exactly the same proportion in which it is smaller or larger than the other; and therefore also the existence of a determined number or ratio a which is the exact square-root of any proposed (positive) number or ratio b. To show this more fully, let A B D be any three given distinct moments, connected by the relations

$$\frac{\mathrm{D}-\mathrm{A}}{\mathrm{B}-\mathrm{A}} = b, \; b > 1, \qquad (214.)$$

which require that the moment B should be situated between A and D; and let C be any fourth moment, lying between B and D, but capable of being chosen as near to B or as near to D as we may desire, in the continuous progression of time. Then the two ratios

$$\frac{\mathrm{C}-\mathrm{A}}{\mathrm{B}-\mathrm{A}} \text{ and } \frac{\mathrm{D}-\mathrm{A}}{\mathrm{C}-\mathrm{A}}$$

will both be positive ratios, and both will be *ratios of largeness*, (that is, each will be a relation of a larger to a smaller step,) which we may denote for abridgement as follows,

$$\frac{\mathrm{C}-\mathrm{A}}{\mathrm{B}-\mathrm{A}} = x, \; \frac{\mathrm{D}-\mathrm{A}}{\mathrm{C}-\mathrm{A}} = y = \mathrm{II}\, x \times b; \qquad (215.)$$

but by choosing the moment C sufficiently near to B we may make the ratio x approach as near as we desire to the ratio of equality denoted by 1, while the ratio y

will tend to the given ratio of largeness denoted by b; results which we may express by the following written sentence,

$$\text{if } \underline{\text{L}}\, \text{C} = \text{B}, \text{ then } \underline{\text{L}}\, x = 1 \text{ and } \underline{\text{L}}\, y = b, \qquad (216.)$$

prefixing the symbol $\underline{\text{L}}$, (namely the initial letter L of the Latin word Limes, distinguished by a bar drawn under it,) to the respective marks of the variable moment C and variable ratios x, y, in order to denote the respective *limits* to which those variables tend, while we vary the selection of one of them, and therefore also of the rest. Again, we may choose the moment C nearer and nearer to D, and then the ratio x will tend to the given ratio of largeness denoted by b, while the ratio y will tend to the ratio of equality; that is,

$$\text{if } \underline{\text{L}}\, \text{C} = \text{D}, \text{ then } \underline{\text{L}}\, x = b, \ \underline{\text{L}}\, y = 1; \qquad (217.)$$

and if we conceive a continuous progression of moments C from B to D, we shall also have a continuous progression of ratios x, determining higher and higher degrees of relative largeness (of the increasing step C − A as compared with the fixed step B − A) from the ratio of equality 1 to the given ratio of largeness b, together with another continuous but opposite progression of ratios y, determining lower and lower degrees of relative largeness (of the fixed step D − A as compared with the increasing step C − A) from the same given ratio of largeness b down to the ratio of equality 1; so that we cannot avoid conceiving the existence of some one determined state of the progression of the moment C, for which the two progressions of ratio *meet*, and for which they give

$$\text{ॻ}\, x \times b = y = x, \text{ that is } \frac{\text{D} - \text{A}}{\text{C} - \text{A}} = \frac{\text{C} - \text{A}}{\text{B} - \text{A}}, \qquad (218.)$$

having given at first $y > x$, and giving afterwards $y < x$. And since, in general,

$$\frac{\text{D} - \text{A}}{\text{C} - \text{A}} \times \frac{\text{C} - \text{A}}{\text{B} - \text{A}} = \frac{\text{D} - \text{A}}{\text{B} - \text{A}}, \text{ that is, } (\text{ॻ}\, x \times b) \times x = b, \qquad (219.)$$

we can and must by (218.) and (214.), conceive the existence of a positive ratio a which shall satisfy the condition (209.), $a \times a = b$, if $b > 1$, that is, we must conceive the existence of a positive square-root of b, if b denote any positive ratio of largeness. A reasoning of an entirely similar kind would prove that we must conceive the existence of a positive square-root of b, when b denotes any positive ratio of smallness, ($b < 1$;) and if b denote the positive ratio of equality, ($b = 1$,) then it evidently has that ratio of equality itself for a positive square-root. We see then by this more full examination what we before assumed to be true, that every positive number or ratio b has a positive (and therefore also a contra-positive) square-root.

And hence we can easily prove another important property of ratios, which has been already mentioned without proof; namely that several ratios can and must be conceived to exist, which are incapable of being expressed under the form of whole or fractional numbers; or, in other words, that every effective step a has other steps *incommensurable* with it; and therefore that when any two distinct moments A and B are given, it is possible to assign (in various ways) a third moment C which shall not be *uniserial* with these two, in the sense of the 8th article, that is, shall not belong in common with them to any one equi-distant series of moments, comprising all the three. For example, the positive square-root of 2, which is evidently intermediate between 1 and 2 in the general progression of numbers, and which therefore is not a whole number, cannot be expressed as a fractional number either; since if it could be put under the fractional form $\frac{n}{m}$, so that

$$\sqrt{2} = \frac{n}{m}, \qquad (220.)$$

we should then have

$$2 = \frac{n}{m} \times \frac{n}{m} = \frac{n \times n}{m \times m}, \qquad (221.)$$

that is,

$$n \times n = 2 \times m \times m; \qquad (222.)$$

but the arithmetical properties of quotities are sufficient to prove that this last equation is impossible, whatever positive whole numbers may be denoted by m and n. And hence, if we imagine that

$$\mathrm{b} = \sqrt{2} \times \mathrm{a}, \quad \mathrm{a} > 0, \qquad (223.)$$

the step b which is a mean proportional between the two effective and co-directional steps a and 2 a (of which the latter is double the former) will be *incommensurable* with the step a (and therefore also with the double step 2 a); that is, we cannot find nor conceive any other step c which shall be a *common measurer* of the steps a and b, so as to satisfy the conditions

$$\mathrm{a} = m\ \mathrm{c}, \quad \mathrm{b} = n\ \mathrm{c}, \qquad (224.)$$

whatever positive or contra-positive whole numbers we may denote by m and n; because, if we could do this, we should then have the relations,

$$\mathrm{b} = \frac{n}{m}\,\mathrm{a}, \quad \sqrt{2} = \frac{n}{m}, \qquad (225.)$$

of which the latter has been shown to be impossible. Hence finally, if A and B be any two distinct moments, and if we choose a third moment C such that

$$\frac{C - A}{B - A} = \sqrt{2}, \qquad (226.)$$

the moment C will not be uniserial with A and B, that is, no one equi-distant series of moments can be imagined, comprising all the three. And all that has here been shown respecting the square-root of two, extends to the square-root of three, and may be illustrated and applied in an infinite variety of other examples. We must then admit the existence of pairs of steps which have no common measurer; and may call the ratio between any two such steps an *incommensurable ratio*, or *incommensurable number*.

More formal proof of the general existence of a determined positive square-root, commensurable or incommensurable, for every determined positive ratio: continuity of progression of the square, and principles connected with this continuity.

26. The existence of these incommensurables, (or the necessity of conceiving them to exist,) is so curious and remarkable a result, that it may be usefully confirmed by an additional proof of the general existence of square-roots of positive ratios, which will also offer an opportunity of considering some other important principles.

The existence of a positive square-root $a = \sqrt{b}$, of any proposed ratio of largeness $b > 1$, was proved in the foregoing article, by the comparison of the two opposite progressions of the two ratios x and ꓤ $x \times b$, from the states $x = 1$, ꓤ $x \times b = b$, for which ꓤ $x \times b > x$, to the states $x = b$, ꓤ $x \times b = 1$, for which ꓤ $x \times b < x$; for this comparison obliged us to conceive the existence of an intermediate state or ratio a between the limits 1 and b, as a *common state* or *state of meeting* of these two opposite progressions, corresponding to the conception of a *moment* at which the decreasing ratio ꓤ $x \times b$ *becomes exactly equal* to the increasing ratio x, having been *previously a greater ratio* (or a ratio of greater relative largeness between steps), and becoming *afterwards a lesser ratio* (or a ratio of less relative largeness). And it was remarked that an exactly similar comparison of two other inverse progressions would prove the existence of a positive square-root $\sqrt{b}$ of any proposed positive ratio b of smallness, $b < 1$, $b > 0$. But instead of thus comparing, with the progression of the positive ratio x, the connected but opposite progression of the connected positive ratio $\mathrm{I\!I}\, x \times b$, and showing that these progressions meet each other in a certain intermediate state or positive ratio a, we might have compared the two connected and not opposite progressions of the two connected positive ratios x and $x \times x$, of which the latter is the square of the former; and might have shown that the square $(= x \times x = x\,x)$ increases *constantly and continuously* with the root $(= x)$, from the state zero, so as to *pass successively through every state* of positive ratio b. To develope this last conception, and to draw from it a more formal (if not a more convincing) proof than that already given, of the necessary existence of a conceivable positive square-root for every conceivable positive number, we shall here lay down a few *Lemmas*, or preliminary and auxiliary propositions.

Lemma I. If $x' \gtreqless x$, and $x > 0$, $x' > 0$, then $x'x' \gtreqless x\,x$; (227.)

that is, the square $x'x'$ of any one positive number or ratio x', is greater than, or equal to, or less than the square xx of any other positive number or ratio x, according as the number x' itself is greater than, or equal to, or less than the number x; one number x' being said to be *greater* or *less* than another number x, when it is on the positive or on the contra-positive side of that other, in the general progression of numbers considered in the 21st article. This Lemma may be easily proved from the conceptions of ratios and of squares; it follows also without difficulty from the theorem of multiplication (200.). And hence we may obviously deduce as a *corollary* of the foregoing Lemma, this converse proposition:

$$\text{if } x'x' \gtreqless x\,x, \text{ and } x > 0,\ x' > 0, \text{ then } x' \gtreqless x; \qquad (228.)$$

that is, if any two proposed positive numbers have positive square-roots, the root of the one number is greater than, or equal to, or less than the root of the other number, according as the former proposed number itself is greater than, or equal to, or less than the latter proposed number.

The foregoing Lemma shows that the square *constantly* increases with the root, from zero up to states indefinitely greater and greater. But to show that this increase is *continuous* as well as constant, and to make more distinct the conception of such continuous increase, these other Lemmas may be added.

Lemma II. If a' and a'' be any two unequal ratios, we can and must conceive the existence of some intermediate ratio a; that is, we can always choose a or conceive it chosen so that

$$a > a', \quad a < a'', \quad \text{if} \quad a'' > a'. \qquad (229.)$$

For then we have the following relation of subsequence between moments,

$$a'' (\mathrm{B}-\mathrm{A})+\mathrm{A} > a' (\mathrm{B}-\mathrm{A})+\mathrm{A}, \text{ if } \mathrm{B} > \mathrm{A}, \qquad (230.)$$

by the very meaning of the relation of subsequence between ratios, $a'' > a'$, as defined in article 21.; and between any two distinct moments it is manifestly possible to insert an intermediate moment, indeed as many such as we may desire: it is, therefore, possible to insert a moment C between the two non-coincident moments

$$a' (\mathrm{B}-\mathrm{A})+\mathrm{A} \text{ and } a'' (\mathrm{B}-\mathrm{A})+\mathrm{A},$$

such that

$$\mathrm{C} > a' (\mathrm{B}-\mathrm{A})+\mathrm{A}, \quad \mathrm{C} < a'' (\mathrm{B}-\mathrm{A})+\mathrm{A}, \text{ if } \mathrm{B} > \mathrm{A}, \; a'' > a'; \qquad (231.)$$

and then if we put, for abridgement,

$$a = \frac{\mathrm{C}-\mathrm{A}}{\mathrm{B}-\mathrm{A}}, \qquad (232.)$$

denoting by a the ratio of the step or interval $\mathrm{C}-\mathrm{A}$ to the step or interval $\mathrm{B}-\mathrm{A}$, we shall have

$$\left.\begin{array}{r} \mathrm{C}=a (\mathrm{B}-\mathrm{A})+\mathrm{A}, \; \mathrm{B} > \mathrm{A}, \\ a (\mathrm{B}-\mathrm{A})+\mathrm{A} > a'(\mathrm{B}-\mathrm{A})+\mathrm{A}, \\ a (\mathrm{B}-\mathrm{A})+\mathrm{A} < a''(\mathrm{B}-\mathrm{A})+\mathrm{A}, \end{array}\right\} \qquad (233.)$$

and therefore finally,

$$a > a', \; a < a'',$$

as was asserted in the Lemma. We see, too, that the ratio a is not determined by the conditions of that Lemma, but that an indefinite variety of ratios may be chosen, which shall all satisfy those conditions.

Corollary. It is possible to choose, or conceive chosen, a ratio a, which shall satisfy all the following conditions,

$$\left.\begin{array}{l} a > a', \; a > b', \; a > c', \ldots \\ a < a'', \; a < b'', \; a < c'', \ldots \end{array}\right\} \qquad (234.)$$

if the least (or hindmost) of the ratios a'', b'', c'', ... be greater (or farther advanced in the general progression of ratio from contra-positive to positive) than the greatest (or foremost in that general progression) of the ratios a', b', c', &c.

For if c'' (for example) be the least or hindmost of the ratios a'', b'', c'',... so that

$$c'' \leqq a'', \quad c'' \leqq b'', \quad c'' \leqq d'', \ldots \qquad (235.)$$

and if b' (for example) be the greatest or foremost of the ratios a', b', c', ... so that

$$b' \geqq a', \quad b' \geqq c', \quad b' \geqq d', \ldots \qquad (236.)$$

(the abridged sign $\leqq$ denoting what might be more fully written thus, " $<$ or $=$", and the other abridged sign $\geqq$ denoting in like manner "$>$ or $=$",) then the conditions (234.) of the Corollary will all be satisfied, if we can satisfy these two conditions,

$$a > b', \quad a < c''; \qquad (237.)$$

and this, by the Lemma, it is possible to do, if we have the relation

$$c'' > b', \qquad (238.)$$

which relation the enunciation of the Corollary supposes to exist.

Remark.—If the ratios $a'\ b'\ c' \ldots a''\ b''\ c'' \ldots$ be all actually given, and therefore limited in number; or if, more generally, the least of the ratios $a''\ b''\ c'' \ldots$ and the greatest of the ratios $a'\ b'\ c' \ldots$ be actually given and determined, so that we have only to choose a ratio a intermediate between two given unequal ratios; we can then make this choice in an indefinite variety of ways, even if it should be farther required that a should be a fractional number $\frac{\nu}{\mu}$, since we saw, in the 8th article, that between any two distinct moments, such as a' (B − A) + A and a'' (B − A) + A, it is possible to insert an indefinite variety of others, such as $\frac{\nu}{\mu}$ (B − A) + A, *uniserial* with the two moments A and B, and giving therefore fractions such as $\frac{\nu}{\mu}$, intermediate (by the 21st article) between the ratios a' and a''. But if, instead of actually knowing the ratios $a'\ b'\ c' \ldots a''\ b''\ c'' \ldots$ themselves, in (234.), we only know a *law* by which we may assign such ratios without end, this law may lead us to conceive new conditions of the form (234.), incompatible with some (and perhaps ultimately with all) of these selections of fractional ratios $\frac{\nu}{\mu}$, although they can never exclude *all ratios a whatever,* unless they be incompatible with each other, that is, unless they fail to possess the relation mentioned in the Corollary. The force of this remark will soon be felt more fully.

Lemma III. If b denote any given positive ratio, whether it be or be not the square of any whole or of any fractional number, it is possible to find, or to conceive as found, one positive ratio a, and only one, which shall satisfy all the conditions of the following forms:

$$a > \frac{n'}{m'}, \quad a < \frac{n''}{m''}, \qquad (239.)$$

$m' \; n' \; m'' \; n''$ denoting here any positive whole numbers whatever, which can be chosen so as to satisfy these relations,

$$\frac{n' \; n'}{m' \; m'} < b, \quad \frac{n'' \; n''}{m'' \; m''} > b. \qquad (240.)$$

For if the proposed ratio b be not the square of any whole or fractional number, then the existence of such a ratio a may be proved from the two preceding Lemmas, or from their Corollaries, by observing that the relations (240.) give

$$\frac{n'' \; n''}{m'' \; m''} > \frac{n' \; n'}{m' \; m'}, \text{ and therefore } \frac{n''}{m''} > \frac{n'}{m'}; \qquad (241.)$$

so that no two conditions of the forms (239.) are incompatible with each other, and there must be *at least one* positive ratio a which satisfies them all. And to prove in the same case that there is *only one* such ratio, or that if any one positive ratio a satisfy all the conditions (239.), no greater ratio c ($> a$) can possibly satisfy all those conditions, we may observe that however little may be the excess $\Theta \, a + c$ of the ratio c over a, this excess may be multiplied by a positive whole number m' so large that the product shall be greater than unity, in such a manner that

$$m' \, (\Theta \, a + c) > 1, \qquad (242.)$$

and therefore

$$\Theta \, a + c > \frac{1}{m'}, \text{ and } c > \frac{1}{m'} + a; \qquad (243.)$$

and that then another positive (or null) whole number n' can be so chosen that

$$\frac{n' \; n'}{m' \; m'} < b, \quad \frac{1 + n'}{m'} \times \frac{1 + n'}{m'} > b, \qquad (244.)$$

with which selection we shall have, by (239.) (240.) (243.),

$$a > \frac{n'}{m'}, \quad c > \frac{1 + n'}{m'}: \qquad (245.)$$

whereas, if c satisfied the conditions (239.) it ought to be less than this fraction $\frac{1 + n'}{m'}$, because the square of this positive fraction is greater by (244.) than the proposed ratio b. In like manner it may be proved that in the other case, when b is the square of a positive fractional or positive whole number $\frac{n}{m}$, one positive ratio a and only one, namely the number $\frac{n}{m}$ itself, will satisfy all the conditions (239.); in both cases, therefore, the Lemma is true: and the consideration of the latter case shows, that, under the conditions (239.),

$$a = \frac{n}{m} \text{ if } b = \frac{n\,n}{m\,m}, \quad \frac{n}{m} > 0. \qquad (240.)$$

In no case do the conditions (239.) exclude *all* ratios a whatever; but except in the case (246.) they *exclude all fractional ratios*: for it will soon be shown that the one ratio a which they do not exclude has its square always $= b$, and must, therefore, be an incommensurable number when b is not the square of any integer or fraction. (Compare the *Remark* annexed to the Corollary of the IInd Lemma.)

Lemma IV. If b' and b'' be any two unequal positive ratios, it is always possible to insert between them an intermediate fractional ratio which shall be itself the square of another fractional ratio $\frac{n}{m}$; that is, we can always find, or conceive found, two positive whole numbers m and n which shall satisfy the two conditions,

$$\frac{n\,n}{m\,m} > b', \quad \frac{n\,n}{m\,m} < b'', \text{ if } b'' > b', \ b' > 0. \qquad (247.)$$

For, by the theorem of multiplication (200.), the square of the fraction $\frac{1+n'}{m}$ may be expressed as follows,

$$\frac{1+n'}{m} \times \frac{1+n'}{m} = \frac{1}{m\,m} + \frac{2\,n'}{m\,m} + \frac{n'\,n'}{m\,m}; \qquad (248.)$$

that is, its excess over the square of the fraction $\frac{n'}{m}$ is $\frac{1}{m\,m} + \frac{2\,n'}{m\,m}$, which is less than $\frac{2}{m} \times \frac{1+n'}{m}$, and constantly increases with the positive whole number n' when the positive whole number m remains unaltered; so that the $1+n'$ squares of fractions with the common denominator m, in the following series,

$$\frac{1}{m} \times \frac{1}{m}, \ \frac{2}{m} \times \frac{2}{m}, \ \frac{3}{m} \times \frac{3}{m}, \ldots \frac{n'}{m} \times \frac{n'}{m}, \ \frac{1+n'}{m} \times \frac{1 \times n'}{m}, \qquad (249.)$$

increase by increasing differences which are each less than $\frac{2}{m} \times \frac{1+n'}{m}$, and therefore than $\frac{1}{k}$, if we choose m and n' so as to satisfy the conditions

$$m = 2\,i\,k, \quad 1 + n' = i\,m, \qquad (250.)$$

i and k being any two positive whole numbers assumed at pleasure: with this choice, therefore, of the numbers m and n', some one (at least) such as $\frac{n\,n}{m\,m}$ among the squares of fractions (249.), that is, some one at least among the following squares of fractions,

$$\frac{1}{2\,i\,k} \times \frac{1}{2\,i\,k}, \frac{2}{2\,i\,k} \times \frac{2}{2\,i\,k}, \frac{3}{2\,i\,k} \times \frac{3}{2\,i\,k}, \ldots \frac{2\,i\,i\,k}{2\,i\,k} \times \frac{2\,i\,i\,k}{2\,i\,k}, \qquad (251.)$$

of which the last is $= i\,i$, must lie between any two proposed unequal positive ratios b' and b'', of which the greater b'' does not exceed that last square $i\,i$, and of which the difference $\Theta\, b' + b''$ is not less than $\frac{1}{k}$; and positive whole numbers i and k can always be so chosen as to satisfy these last conditions, however great the proposed ratio b'' may be, and however little may be its excess $\Theta\, b' + b''$ over the other proposed ratio b'.

27. With these preparations it is easy to prove, in a new and formal way, the existence of *one determined positive square root* $\sqrt{b}$ for every proposed positive ratio b, whether that ratio b be or be not the square of any whole or of any fractional number; for we can now prove this *Theorem:*

The square $a\,a$ of the determined positive ratio a, of which ratio the existence was shown in the IIId. Lemma, is equal to the proposed positive ratio b in the same Lemma; that is,

$$\left.\begin{array}{c} \text{if } a > \frac{n'}{m'} \text{ whenever } \frac{n'\,n'}{m'\,m'} < b, \\ \text{and } a < \frac{n''}{m''} \text{ whenever } \frac{n''\,n''}{m''\,m''} > b, \\ \text{then } a\,a = b,\ a = \sqrt{b}, \end{array}\right\} \qquad (252.)$$

$m'\,n'\,m''\,n''$ being any positive whole numbers which satisfy the conditions here mentioned, and b being any determined positive ratio.

For if the square $a\,a$ of the positive ratio a, determined by these conditions, could be greater than the proposed positive ratio b, it would be possible, by the IVth Lemma, to insert between them some positive fraction which would be the square of another positive fraction $\frac{n}{m}$; that is, we could choose m and n so that

$$\frac{nn}{mm} > b,\ \frac{nn}{mm} < aa: \qquad (253.)$$

and then, by the Corollary to the Ist Lemma, and by the conditions (252.), we should be conducted to the two following incompatible relations,

$$\frac{n}{m} < a, \; a < \frac{n}{m}. \qquad (254.)$$

A similar absurdity would result, if we were to suppose $a\,a$ less than b; $a\,a$ must therefore be equal to b, that is, the theorem is true. It has, indeed, been here assumed as evident, that every determined positive ratio a has a determined positive square $a\,a$; which is included in this more general but equally evident principle, that any two determined positive ratios or numbers have a determined positive product.

We find it, therefore, proved, by the most minute and rigorous examination, that if we conceive any positive ratio x or a to increase constantly and continuously from 0, we must conceive its square $x\,x$ or aa to increase constantly and continuously with it, so as to pass successively but only once through every state of positive ratio b: and therefore that every determined positive ratio b has one determined positive square root $\sqrt{b}$, which will be commensurable or incommensurable, according as b can or cannot be expressed as the square of a fraction. When b cannot be so expressed, it is still possible to *approximate in fractions* to the incommensurable square root $\sqrt{b}$, by choosing successively larger and larger positive denominators, and then seeking for every such denominator m' the corresponding positive numerator n' which satisfies the two conditions (244.); for although every fraction thus found will be less than the sought root $\sqrt{b}$, yet the error, or the positive correction which must be added to it in order to produce the accurate root $\sqrt{b}$, is less than the reciprocal of the denominator m', and therefore may be made as little different as we please from 0, (though it can never be made exactly $= 0$,) by choosing that denominator large enough. This process of approximation to an incommensurable root $\sqrt{b}$ is capable, therefore, of an indefinitely great, though never of a perfect accuracy; and using the notation already given for *limits*, we may write

$$\sqrt{b} = \underline{\mathrm{L}}\, \frac{n'}{m'}, \text{ if } \frac{n'\,n'}{m'\,m'} < b, \; \frac{1+n'}{m'} \times \frac{1+n'}{m'} > b, \qquad (255.)$$

and may think of the incommensurable root as the *limit* of the varying fractional number.

The only additional remark which need be made, at present, on the subject of the progression of the square $x\,x$, or $a\,a$, as depending on the progression of the root x, or a, is that since (by the 24th article) the square remains positive and unchanged when the root is changed from positive to contra-positive, in such a manner that

$$\Theta a \times \Theta a = a \times a, \qquad (256.)$$

the square aa must be conceived as *first* constantly and continuously *decreasing* or *retrograding* towards 0, and *afterwards* constantly and continuously *increasing* or *advancing* from 0, if the root a be conceived as constantly and continuously increasing or advancing, in the general progression of ratio, from states indefinitely far from 0 on the contra-positive side, to other states indefinitely far from 0, but on the positive side in the progression.

On Continued Analogies, or Series of Proportional Steps; and on Powers, and Roots, and Logarithms of Ratios.

28. Four effective steps $\mathfrak{a}\ \mathfrak{b}\ \mathfrak{b}'\ \mathfrak{b}''$ may be said to form a continued analogy or continued proportion, $\mathfrak{a}$ and $\mathfrak{b}''$ being the extremes, and $\mathfrak{b}$ and $\mathfrak{b}'$ the means, when they are connected by one common ratio in the following manner:

$$\frac{\mathfrak{b}''}{\mathfrak{b}'} = \frac{\mathfrak{b}'}{\mathfrak{b}} = \frac{\mathfrak{b}}{\mathfrak{a}}; \qquad (257.)$$

and if we denote for abridgement this common ratio by a, we may write

$$\mathfrak{b} = a \times \mathfrak{a},\ \mathfrak{b}' = a \times a \times \mathfrak{a},\ \mathfrak{b}'' = a \times a \times a \times \mathfrak{a}. \qquad (258.)$$

Reciprocally, when $\mathfrak{b}\ \mathfrak{b}'\ \mathfrak{b}''$ can be thus expressed, the four steps $\mathfrak{a}\ \mathfrak{b}\ \mathfrak{b}'\ \mathfrak{b}''$ compose a continued *analogy;* and it is clear that if the first extreme step $\mathfrak{a}$ and the common ratio a be given, the other steps can be deduced by the multiplications (258.) It is easy also to perceive, that if the two extremes $\mathfrak{a}$ and $\mathfrak{b}''$ be given, the two means $\mathfrak{b}$ and $\mathfrak{b}'$ may be conceived to be determined (as necessarily connected with these) in one and in only one way; and thus that the insertion of *two mean proportionals* between two given effective steps, is never impossible nor ambiguous, like the insertion of a single mean proportional. In fact, it follows from the theorems of multiplication that the product $a \times a \times a$, which may be called the *cube* of the number or ratio a, is not obliged (like the square $a \times a$) to be always a positive ratio, but is positive or contra-positive according as a itself (which may be called the *cube-root* of this product

$a \times a \times a$) is positive or contra-positive; and on examining the law of its progression, (as we lately examined the law of the progression of the square,) we find that the cube $a \times a \times a$ increases constantly and continuously with its cube-root a from states indefinitely far from zero, on the contra-positive side, to states indefinitely far advanced on the positive side of zero, in the general progression of ratio, so as to pass successively but only once through every state of contra-positive or positive ratio, instead of first decreasing or retrograding, and afterwards increasing or advancing, like the square. Thus every ratio has one and only one cube-root, (commensurable or incommensurable,) although a ratio has sometimes two square-roots and sometimes none, according as it is positive or contra-positive; and when the two extreme effective steps a and b'' of the continued analogy (257.) are given, we can always conceive the cube-root a of their ratio $\frac{\mathrm{b}''}{\mathrm{a}}$ determined, and hence the two mean steps or mean proportionals of the analogy, b and b'.

29. In general, as we conceived a continued analogy or *series of equi-distant moments*, generated from a single standard moment A, by the *repetition* of a forward *step* a and of a backward step $\Theta\,\mathrm{a}$; so we may now conceive, as another sort of continued analogy, a *series of proportional steps*, generated from a single standard (effective) step a, by the *repetition* of the *act of multiplication* which corresponds to and is determined by some one multiplier or ratio $a\,(\neq 0)$, and of the inverse or reciprocal act of multiplication determined by the reciprocal multiplier or ratio ꓤa: namely, the following series of proportional steps,

$$\ldots ꓤa \times ꓤa \times ꓤa \times \mathrm{a},\ ꓤa \times ꓤa \times \mathrm{a},\ ꓤa \times \mathrm{a},\ \mathrm{a},\ a \times \mathrm{a},\ a \times a \times \mathrm{a},\ a \times a \times a \times \mathrm{a}, \ldots \qquad (259.)$$

which may also be thus denoted,

$$\ldots ꓤ(a\,a\,a) \times \mathrm{a},\ ꓤ(a\,a) \times \mathrm{a},\ ꓤa \times \mathrm{a},\ 1 \times \mathrm{a},\ a \times \mathrm{a},\ a\,a \times \mathrm{a},\ a\,a\,a \times \mathrm{a}, \ldots \qquad (260.)$$

and in which we may consider the system or series of ratios or multipliers,

$$\ldots ꓤ(a\,a\,a),\ ꓤ(a\,a),\ ꓤa,\ 1,\ a,\ a\,a,\ a\,a\,a, \ldots \qquad (261.)$$

to be a *system generated* from the original ratio or multiplier a, by a *system of acts* of generation having all one common character: as we before considered the system of multiple steps (98.),

$$\ldots \Theta\mathrm{a} + \Theta\mathrm{a} + \Theta\mathrm{a},\ \Theta\mathrm{a} + \Theta\mathrm{a},\ \Theta\mathrm{a},\ 0,\ \mathrm{a},\ \mathrm{a} + \mathrm{a},\ \mathrm{a} + \mathrm{a} + \mathrm{a}, \ldots$$

to be a system of steps generated from the original step a by a system of acts of generation to which we gave the common name of acts of multiplying.

In conformity with this conception, we may call the original ratio a the *base* of the system of ratios (261.) and may call those ratios by the common name of *powers* of that common base, and say that they are (or may be) formed by acts of *powering* it. And to distinguish any one such power, or one such act of powering, from all the other powers in the system, or from all the other acts of powering, we may employ the aid of *determining numbers*, ordinal or cardinal, in a manner analogous to that explained in the 13th article for a system of multiple steps. Thus, we may call the ratios a, $a\,a$, $a\,a\,a$, ... by the common name of *positive powers* of the base a, and may distinguish them by the special ordinal names *first, second, third*, &c.; so that the ratio a is, in this view, its own first positive power; the second positive power is the square $a\,a$, and the third positive power is the cube. Again, we may call the ratio 1, which immediately precedes these positive powers in the series, the *zero-power* of the base a, by analogy to the zero-multiple in the series of multiple steps, which immediately preceded in that series the system of positive multiples; and the ratios $\mathfrak{u}\,a$, $\mathfrak{u}\,(a\,a)$, $\mathfrak{u}\,(a\,a\,a)$, ... which precede this zero-power 1 in the series of powers (261.), may be called, by the same analogy, from their order of position, *contra-positive powers* of a, so that the reciprocal $\mathfrak{u}\,a$ of any ratio a is the *first contra-positive power* of that ratio, the reciprocal $\mathfrak{u}\,(a\,a)$ of its square is its second contra-positive power, and so on. We may also distinguish the several corresponding acts of powering by the corresponding cardinal numbers, positive, or contra-positive, or null, and may say (for example) that the third positive power $a\,a\,a$ is formed from the base a by the act of *powering by positive three;* that the second contra-positive power $\mathfrak{u}\,(a\,a)$ is formed from the same base a by *powering by contra-positive two;* and that the zero-power 1 is (or may be) formed from a by powering that base by the null cardinal or number *none*. In written symbols, answering to these thoughts and names, we may denote the *series of powers* (261.), and the *series of proportional steps* (260.), as follows,

$$\ldots\, a^{\ominus 3},\ a^{\ominus 2},\ a^{\ominus 1},\ a^{0},\ a^{1},\ a^{2},\ a^{3},\ \ldots \qquad (262.)$$

and

$$\ldots\, a^{\ominus 3}\times\mathfrak{a},\ a^{\ominus 2}\times\mathfrak{a},\ a^{\ominus 1}\times\mathfrak{a},\ a^{0}\times\mathfrak{a},\ a^{1}\times\mathfrak{a},\ a^{2}\times\mathfrak{a},\ a^{3}\times\mathfrak{a},\ \ldots \qquad (263.)$$

in which

$$a^{0}=1, \qquad (264.)$$

and

$$\left.\begin{array}{ll} a^{1}=a, & a^{\ominus 1}=\mathfrak{u}\,a, \\ a^{2}=a\,a, & a^{\ominus 2}=\mathfrak{u}\,(a\,a), \\ a^{3}=a\,a\,a, & a^{\ominus 3}=\mathfrak{u}\,(a\,a\,a), \\ \&c. & \&c. \end{array}\right\} \qquad (265.)$$

And we may give the name of *exponents* or *logarithms* to the determining numbers, ordinal or cardinal,

$$\ldots \ominus 3,\ \ominus 2,\ \ominus 1,\ 0,\ 1,\ 2,\ 3,\ \ldots\ldots \qquad (266.)$$

which answer the question "*which in order* is the Power?" or this other question "*Have any* (effective) acts of multiplication, equivalent or reciprocal to the original act of multiplying by the given ratio a, been combined to produce the act of multiplying by the Power; and if any, then *How many*, and *In which direction*, that is, whether are they similar or opposite in effect, (as enlarging or diminishing the step on which they are performed,) to that original act?" Thus 2 is the logarithm of the square or second power $a\,a$, when compared with the base a; 3 is the logarithm of the cube $a\,a\,a$, 1 is the logarithm of the base a itself, $\ominus$ 1 is the logarithm of the reciprocal $\text{ɪ}\, a$, and 0 is the logarithm of the ratio 1 considered as the zero-power of a.

With these conceptions and notations of powers and logarithms, we can easily prove the relation

$$a^{\nu} \times a^{\mu} = a^{\nu+\mu}, \qquad (267.)$$

for any integer logarithms μ and ν, whether positive, or contra-positive, or null; and this other connected relation

$$b^{\nu} = a^{\nu \times \mu} \text{ if } b = a^{\mu}; \qquad (268.)$$

which may be thus expressed in words: "Any two powers of any common base may be multiplied together by adding their logarithms," and "Any proposed power may be powered by any proposed whole number, by multiplying its logarithm by that number," if the sum of the two proposed logarithms in the first case, or the multiple of the proposed logarithm in the second case, be employed as a new logarithm, to form a new power of the original base or ratio; the logarithms here considered being all whole numbers.

30. The act of passing from a base to a power, is connected with an inverse or reciprocal act of returning from the power to the base; and the conceptions of both these acts are included in the more comprehensive conception of the act of passing from any one to any other of the ratios of the series (261.) or (262.). This act of passing from any one power a^{μ} to any other power a^{ν} of a common base a, may be still called in general an act of *powering*; and more particularly, (keeping up the analogy to the language already employed in the theory of multiple steps,) it may be called the act of *powering by the fractional number* $\frac{\nu}{\mu}$. By the same analogy of

definition, this fractional number may be called the *logarithm* of the resulting power, and the power itself may be denoted in written symbols as follows,

$$(a^\mu)^{\frac{\nu}{\mu}} = a^\nu, \qquad (269.)$$

or thus,

$$c = b^{\frac{\nu}{\mu}}, \text{ if } b = a^\mu, \ c = a^\nu. \qquad (270.)$$

(The analogous formula (121.) ought to have been printed $c = \frac{\nu}{\mu} b$, and not $c = \frac{\nu}{\mu} a$, when $b = \mu \times a$, $c = \nu \times a$.)

In the particular case when the numerator ν is 1, and when, therefore, we have to power by the reciprocal of a whole number, we may call the result $(a^\mu)^{\frac{1}{\mu}}$, that is a^1, $= a$, a *root* or more fully *the* μ*'th root* of the power or ratio a^μ; and we may call the corresponding act of powering, an *extraction of the* μ*'th root,* or a *rooting by the (whole) number* μ. Thus, to power any proposed ratio b by the reciprocal number $\frac{1}{2}$ or $\frac{1}{3}$, is to extract the second or the third root, that is, (by what has been already shown,) the square-root or the cube-root, of b, or to root the proposed ratio b by the number 2 or 3; and in conformity with this last mode of expression, the following notation may be employed,

$$a = \sqrt[\mu]{b} \text{ when } b = a^\mu, \ a = b^{\frac{1}{\mu}}: \qquad (271.)$$

so that a square-root $\sqrt{b}$ may also be denoted by the symbol $\sqrt[2]{b}$, and the cube-root of b may be denoted by $\sqrt[3]{b}$. And whereas we saw, in considering square-roots that a contra-positive ratio $b<0$ has no square-root, and that a positive ratio $b>0$ has two square-roots, one positive $= \sqrt{b}$ and the other contra-positive $= \ominus \sqrt{b}$, of which each has its square $= b$; we may consider the new sign $b^{\frac{1}{2}}$ or $\sqrt[2]{b}$ as denoting indifferently either of these two roots, reserving the old sign $\sqrt{b}$ to denote specially that one of them which is positive, and the other old sign $\ominus \sqrt{b}$ to denote specially that one of them which is contra-positive. Thus $\sqrt{b}$ and $\ominus \sqrt{b}$ shall still remain determinate signs, implying each a determinate ratio, (when $b>0$,) while $\sqrt[2]{b}$ and $b^{\frac{1}{2}}$ shall be used as ambiguous signs, susceptible each of two different meanings. But $\sqrt[3]{b}$ is a determinate sign, because a ratio has only one cube-root. In general, an *even* root, such as the second, fourth, or sixth, of a proposed ratio b, is ambiguous if that ratio be positive, and impossible if b be contra-positive; because an even power, or a power with an even integer for its logarithm, is always a positive ratio, whether the base be positive or contra-positive: but an *odd* root, such as the third or fifth, is always possible and determinate.

31. It may, however, be useful to show more distinctly, by a method analogous to that

of the 26th and 27th articles, that for any proposed positive ratio b whatever, and for any positive whole number m, it is possible to determine, or conceive determined, one positive ratio a, and only one, which shall have its m'th power $=b$; and for this purpose to show that the power a^m increases constantly and continuously from zero with a, so as to pass successively, but only once, through every state of positive ratio b. On examining the proof already given of this property, in the particular case of the power a^2, we see that in order to extend that proof to the more general case of the power a^m, we have only to generalise, as follows, the Ist, IIId, and IVth Lemmas, and the Corollary of the Ist, with the Theorem resulting from all four, retaining the IInd Lemma.

Vth *Lemma*: (generalised from Ist.)

$$\text{If } y \gtreqless x, \text{ and } x>0,\ y>0, \text{ then } y^m \gtreqless x^m. \qquad (272.)$$

When $m=1$, this Lemma is evident, because the first powers y^1 and x^1 coincide with the ratios y and x. When $m>1$, the Lemma may be easily deduced from the conceptions of ratios, and of powers with positive integer exponents; it may also be proved by observing that the difference $\Theta\, x^m + y^m$, between the powers x^m and y^m, in which the symbol $\Theta\, x^m$ denotes the same thing as if we had written more fully $\Theta\,(x^m)$, and which may be obtained in one way by the subtraction of x^m from y^m, may also be obtained in another way by multiplication from the difference $\Theta\, x+y$ as follows:

$$\Theta\, x^m + y^m = (\Theta\, x + y) \times (x^{\Theta 1+m} y^0 + x^{\Theta 2+m} y^1 + \ldots + x^1 y^{\Theta 2+m} + x^0 y^{\Theta 1+m}), \quad (273.)$$

and is, therefore, positive, or contra-positive, or null, according as the difference $\Theta\, x+y$ of the positive ratios x and y themselves is positive, or contra-positive, or null, because the other factor of the product (273.) is positive. For example,

$$\Theta\, x^3 + y^3 = (\Theta\, x + y) \times (x^2 + x\,y + y^2); \qquad (274.)$$

and, therefore, when x and y and consequently $x^2+x\,y+y^2$ are positive, the difference $\Theta\, x^3+y^3$ and the difference $\Theta\, x+y$ are positive, or contra-positive, or null together.

As a *Corollary* of this Lemma, we see that, conversely,

$$\text{if } y^m \gtreqless x^m, \text{ and } x>0,\ y>0, \text{ then } y \gtreqless x. \qquad (275.)$$

Thus, the power x^m and the root x increase *constantly* together, when both are positive ratios.

The *logic* of this last deduction, of the Corollary (275.) from the Lemma (272.), must not be confounded with that erroneous form of argument which infers the truth of the antecedent of a true hypothetical proposition from the truth of the consequent; that is, with the too common *sophism:* If A be true then B is true; but B is true, therefore A is true. The Lemma (272.) asserts three hypothetical propositions, which are tacitly supposed to be each transformed, or logically converted, according to this *valid* principle, that the falsehood of the consequent of a true hypothetical proposition infers the falsehood of the antecedent; or according to this just formula: If A were true then B would be true; but B is false, therefore A is not true. Applying this just principle to each of the three hypothetical propositions of the Lemma, we are entitled to infer, by the general principles of Logic, these three converse hypothetical propositions:

$$\left.\begin{array}{l} \text{if } y^m \not> x^m, \text{ then } y \not> x; \\ \text{if } y^m \neq x^m, \text{ then } y \neq x; \\ \text{if } y^m \not< x^m, \text{ then } y \not< x; \end{array}\right\} \qquad (276.)$$

x and y being here any positive ratios, and m any positive whole number, and the signs $\not>$ $\not<$ denoting respectively "not >" and "not <" as the sign $\neq$ denotes "not =". And if, to the propositions (276.), we join this principle of intuition in Algebra, as the Science of Pure Time, that a variable moment B must either follow, or coincide with, or precede a given or variable moment A, but cannot do two of these three things at once, and therefore (by the 21st article) that a variable ratio y must also bear one but only one of these three ordinal relations to a given or variable ratio x, which shows that

$$\left.\begin{array}{l} \text{when } y^m > x^m, \text{ then } y^m \neq x^m \text{ and } y^m \not< x^m, \\ \text{when } y^m = x^m, \text{ then } y^m \not< x^m \text{ and } y^m \not> x^m, \\ \text{when } y^m < x^m, \text{ then } y^m \not> x^m \text{ and } y^m \neq x^m, \end{array}\right\} \qquad (277.)$$

and that

$$\left.\begin{array}{l} \text{when } y \neq x \text{ and } y \not< x, \text{ then } y > x, \\ \text{when } y \not< x \text{ and } y \not> x, \text{ then } y = x, \\ \text{when } y \not> x \text{ and } y \neq x, \text{ then } y < x, \end{array}\right\} \qquad (278.)$$

we find finally that the Corollary (275.) is true. The same logic was tacitly employed in deducing the Corollary of the Ist Lemma, in the hope that it would be mentally supplied by the attentive reader. It has now been stated expressly, lest any should confound it with that dangerous and common fallacy, of inferring, in Pure Science, the necessary truth of a premiss in an argument, from the known truth of the conclusion.

Resuming the more mathematical part of the research, we may next establish this

VIth *Lemma* (generalised from IIId): There exists one positive ratio a, and only one, which satisfies all the following conditions,

$$\left.\begin{array}{l} a > \frac{n'}{m'} \text{ whenever } \left(\frac{n'}{m'}\right)^m < b, \\ a < \frac{n''}{m''} \text{ whenever } \left(\frac{n''}{m''}\right)^m > b\,; \end{array}\right\} \qquad (279.)$$

b being any given positive ratio, and m any given positive whole number, while m' n' m'' n'' are also positive but variable whole numbers. The proof of this Lemma is so like that of the IIId, that it need not be written here; and it shows that in the particular case when the given ratio b is the mth power of a positive fraction $\frac{n_{\prime}}{m_{\prime}}$, then a is that fraction itself. In general, it will soon be shown that under the conditions of this Lemma the mth power of a is b.

VIIth *Lemma* (generalised from IVth). It is always possible to find, or to conceive as found, two positive whole numbers $m_{\prime}$ and $n_{\prime}$, which shall satisfy the two conditions

$$\left(\frac{n_{\prime}}{m_{\prime}}\right)^m > b', \quad \left(\frac{n_{\prime}}{m_{\prime}}\right)^m < b'', \text{ if } b'' > b', \; b' > 0, \qquad (280.)$$

m being any given positive whole number; that is, we can insert between any two unequal positive ratios b' and b'' an intermediate fractional ratio which is itself the mth power of a fraction.

For, when $m = 1$, this Lemma reduces itself to the IInd; and when $m > 1$, the theorem (273.) shows that the excess of $\left(\frac{1+n}{m_{\prime}}\right)^m$ over $\left(\frac{n}{m_{\prime}}\right)^m$ may be expressed as follows;

$$\Theta \left(\frac{n}{m_{\prime}}\right)^m + \left(\frac{1+n}{m_{\prime}}\right)^m = \frac{1}{m_{\prime}} \times p, \qquad (281.)$$

in which

$$p = \left(\frac{n}{m_{\prime}}\right)^{\Theta 1+m} + \left(\frac{n}{m_{\prime}}\right)^{\Theta 2+m}\left(\frac{1+n}{m_{\prime}}\right) + \left(\frac{n}{m_{\prime}}\right)^{\Theta 3+m}\left(\frac{1+n}{m_{\prime}}\right)^2$$
$$+ \ldots + \left(\frac{n}{m_{\prime}}\right)^2 \left(\frac{1+n}{m_{\prime}}\right)^{\Theta 3+m} + \frac{n}{m_{\prime}} \left(\frac{1+n}{m_{\prime}}\right)^{\Theta 2+m} + \left(\frac{1+n}{m_{\prime}}\right)^{\Theta 1+m}; \qquad (282.)$$

for example, when $m=3$, the excess of the cube $\left(\frac{1+n}{m_,}\right)^3$ over the cube $\left(\frac{n}{m_,}\right)^3$, is

$$\Theta\left(\frac{n}{m_,}\right)^3+\left(\frac{1+n}{m_,}\right)^3=\frac{1}{m_,}\times\left\{\left(\frac{n}{m_,}\right)^2+\frac{n}{m_,}\,\frac{1+n}{m_,}+\left(\frac{1+n}{m_,}\right)^2\right\}. \qquad (283.)$$

In general, the number of the *terms* (or added parts) in the expression (282.), is m, and they are all unequal, the least being $\left(\frac{n}{m_,}\right)^{\Theta 1+m}$, and the greatest being $\left(\frac{1+n}{m_,}\right)^{\Theta 1+m}$; their sum, therefore, is less than the mth multiple of this greatest term, that is,

$$p<m\times\left(\frac{1+n}{m_,}\right)^{\Theta 1+m}, \qquad (284.)$$

and therefore the excess (281.) is subject to the corresponding condition

$$\Theta\left(\frac{n}{m_,}\right)^m+\left(\frac{1+n}{m_,}\right)^m<\frac{m}{m_,}\left(\frac{1+n}{m_,}\right)^{\Theta 1+m}; \qquad (285.)$$

for example,

$$\Theta\left(\frac{n}{m_,}\right)^3+\left(\frac{1+n}{m_,}\right)^3<\frac{3}{m_,}\left(\frac{1+n}{m_,}\right)^2. \qquad (286.)$$

However this excess (281.) increases constantly with n, when $m_,$ remains unaltered, because p so increases; so that the $1+n$ fractions of the series

$$\left(\frac{1}{m_,}\right)^m,\ \left(\frac{2}{m_,}\right)^m,\ \left(\frac{3}{m_,}\right)^m,\ \dots\left(\frac{1+n}{m_,}\right)^m, \qquad (287.)$$

increase by increasing differences, (or advance by increasing intervals,) which are each less than $\frac{m}{m_,}\cdot\left(\frac{1+n}{m_,}\right)^{\Theta 1+m}$, and therefore than $\frac{1}{k}$, if we choose $m_,$ and n so as to satisfy the conditions

$$1+n=i\,m_,,\quad m_,=k\,m\times i^{\Theta 1+m}=\frac{k\,m\,i^m}{i}, \qquad (288.)$$

i and k being any two positive whole numbers assumed at pleasure; with this choice, therefore, of the numbers $m_,$ and n, some one (at least), such as $\left(\frac{n_,}{m_,}\right)^m$, of the series of powers of fractions (287.), of which the last is $=i^m$, will fall between any two proposed unequal positive ratios b' and b'', if the greater b'' does not exceed that last power i^m, and if the difference $\Theta\, b'+b''$ is not less than $\frac{1}{k}$; and these conditions can be always satisfied by a suitable choice of the whole numbers i and k, however large may be the given greater positive ratio b'', and however little may be its given excess over the lesser positive ratio b'.

Hence, finally, this Theorem:

$$\left.\begin{array}{c} \text{If } a > \frac{n'}{m'}, \text{ and } a < \frac{n''}{m''}, \\ \text{whenever } \left(\frac{n'}{m'}\right)^m < b, \left(\frac{n''}{m''}\right)^m > b, \\ \text{then } a^m = b, \ a = \sqrt[m]{b} = b^{\frac{1}{m}}; \end{array}\right\} \quad (289.)$$

b denoting any given positive ratio, and m any given positive whole number, while $m'\ n'\ m''\ n''$ are any arbitrary positive whole numbers which satisfy these conditions, and a is another positive ratio which the VIth Lemma shows to be determined.

For if a^m could be $> b$, we could, by the VIIth Lemma, insert between them a positive fraction of the form $\left(\frac{n_{,}}{m_{,}}\right)^m$, such that

$$\left(\frac{n_{,}}{m_{,}}\right)^m > b, \ \left(\frac{n_{,}}{m_{,}}\right)^m < a^m; \qquad (290.)$$

and then by the Corollary of the Vth Lemma, and by the conditions (289.), we should deduce the two incompatible relations

$$\frac{n_{,}}{m_{,}} < a, \ a < \frac{n_{,}}{m_{,}}, \qquad (291.)$$

which would be absurd. A similar absurdity would follow from supposing that a^m could be less than b; a^m must therefore be $= b$, that is, the Theorem is true. It has, indeed, been all along assumed as evident that every determined positive ratio a has a determined positive m^{th} power a^m, when m is a positive whole number; which is included in this more general but also evident principle, that any m determined positive ratios or numbers have a determined positive product.

Every positive ratio b has therefore one, and only one, positive ratio a for its mth root, which is commensurable or incommensurable, according as b can or cannot be put under the form $\left(\frac{n_{,}}{m_{,}}\right)^m$; but which, when incommensurable, may be theoretically conceived as the accurate limit of a variable fraction,

$$a = \sqrt[m]{b} = \mathrm{L}\frac{n'}{m'}, \text{ if } \left(\frac{n'}{m'}\right)^m < b, \left(\frac{1+n'}{m'}\right)^m > b, \qquad (292.)$$

and may be practically approached to, by determining such fractions $\frac{n'}{m'}$, with larger and larger whole numbers m' and n' for their denominators and numerators. And whether m be odd or even, we see that the power a^m increases *continuously* (as well as constantly) with its positive root or base a, from zero up to states indefinitely greater and greater. But if this root, or base, or ratio a be conceived to advance constantly and continuously from states indefinitely far from zero on the contra-positive side to states indefinitely far upon the positive side, then the power a^m will either advance constantly and continuously likewise, though not with the same quickness, from contra-positive to positive states, or else will first constantly and continuously retrograde to zero, and afterwards advance from zero, remaining always positive, according as the positive exponent or logarithm m is an odd or an even integer. It is understood that for any such positive exponent m,

$$0^m = 0, \qquad (293.)$$

the powers of 0 with positive integer exponents being considered as all themselves equal to 0, because the repeated multiplication by this null ratio generates from any one effective step a the series of proportional steps,

$$\mathrm{a},\ 0 \times \mathrm{a} = 0,\ 0 \times 0 \times \mathrm{a} = 0,\ \ldots, \qquad (294.)$$

which may be continued indefinitely *in one direction*, and in which all steps after the first are null; although we were obliged to exclude the consideration of such null ratios in forming the series (259.) because we wished to continue that series of steps indefinitely in two opposite directions.

32. We are now prepared to discuss completely the meaning, or meanings, if any, which ought to be assigned to any proposed symbol of the class $b^{\frac{\nu}{\mu}}$, b denoting any proposed ratio, and μ and ν any proposed whole numbers. By the 30th article, the symbol $b^{\frac{\nu}{\mu}}$ denotes generally the ν'th power of a ratio a of which b is the μ'th power; or, in other words, the νth power of a μth root of b; so that the mental operation of passing from the ratio b to the ratio $b^{\frac{\nu}{\mu}}$, is compounded, (when it can be performed at all,) of the two operations of first rooting by the one whole number μ, and then powering by the other whole number ν: and we may write,

$$b^{\frac{\nu}{\mu}} = (\sqrt[\mu]{b})^{\nu} = (b^{\frac{1}{\mu}})^{\nu}. \qquad (295.)$$

The ratio b, and the whole numbers μ and ν, may each be either positive, or contra-positive, or null; and thus there arise many cases, which may be still farther subdivided, by distinguishing between odd and even values of the positive or contra-positive whole numbers. For, if we suppose that B denotes a positive ratio, and that m and n denote positive whole numbers, we may then suppose

$$\left.\begin{array}{l} b=\mathrm{B}, \text{ or } b=0, \text{ or } b=\Theta\,\mathrm{B}, \\ \mu=m, \text{ or } \mu=0, \text{ or } \mu=\Theta\,m, \\ \nu=n, \text{ or } \nu=0, \text{ or } \nu=\Theta\,n, \end{array}\right\} \qquad (296.)$$

and thus shall obtain the twenty-seven cases following,

$$\left.\begin{array}{lll} \mathrm{B}^{\frac{n}{m}}, & \mathrm{B}^{\frac{0}{m}}, & \mathrm{B}^{\frac{\Theta n}{m}} \\ \mathrm{B}^{\frac{n}{0}}, & \mathrm{B}^{\frac{0}{0}}, & \mathrm{B}^{\frac{\Theta n}{0}} \\ \mathrm{B}^{\frac{n}{\Theta m}}, & \mathrm{B}^{\frac{0}{\Theta m}}, & \mathrm{B}^{\frac{\Theta n}{\Theta m}} \end{array}\right\} \qquad (297.)$$

$$\left.\begin{array}{lll} 0^{\frac{n}{m}}, & 0^{\frac{0}{m}}, & 0^{\frac{\Theta n}{m}}, \\ 0^{\frac{n}{0}}, & 0^{\frac{0}{0}}, & 0^{\frac{\Theta n}{0}}, \\ 0^{\frac{n}{\Theta m}}, & 0^{\frac{0}{\Theta m}}, & 0^{\frac{\Theta n}{\Theta m}}, \end{array}\right\} \qquad (298.)$$

$$\left.\begin{array}{lll} (\Theta\,\mathrm{B})^{\frac{n}{m}}, & (\Theta\,\mathrm{B})^{\frac{0}{m}}, & (\Theta\,\mathrm{B})^{\frac{\Theta n}{m}}, \\ (\Theta\,\mathrm{B})^{\frac{n}{0}}, & (\Theta\,\mathrm{B})^{\frac{0}{0}}, & (\Theta\,\mathrm{B})^{\frac{\Theta n}{0}}, \\ (\Theta\,\mathrm{B})^{\frac{n}{\Theta m}}, & (\Theta\,\mathrm{B})^{\frac{0}{\Theta m}}, & (\Theta\,\mathrm{B})^{\frac{\Theta n}{\Theta m}}, \end{array}\right\} \qquad (299.)$$

which we may still farther sub-divide by putting m and n under the forms

$$\left.\begin{array}{l} m=2\,i, \text{ or } m=\Theta\,1+2\,i, \\ n=2\,k, \text{ or } n=\Theta\,1+2\,k, \end{array}\right\} \qquad (300.)$$

in which i and k themselves denote positive whole numbers. But, various as these cases are, the only difficulty in discussing them arises from the occurrence, in some, of the ratio or number 0; and to remove this difficulty, we may lay down the following rules, deduced from the foregoing principles.

To power the ratio 0 by any positive whole number m, gives, by (293.), the ratio 0 as the result. This ratio 0 is, therefore, at least *one* m'th root of 0; and since no positive or contra-positive ratio can thus give 0 when powered by any positive whole number, we see that the *only* m'th root of 0 is 0 itself. Thus,

$$0^{\frac{1}{m}}=0, \qquad (301.)$$

and generally,

$$0^{\frac{n}{m}} = 0. \qquad (302.)$$

To power any positive ratio a, whether positive, or contra-positive, or null, by the number or logarithm 0, may be considered to give 1 as the result; because we can always construct at least this series of proportional steps, beginning with any one effective step $\mathbf{a}$, and proceeding indefinitely in one direction:

$$1 \times \mathbf{a}, \; a \times \mathbf{a}, \; a \times a \times \mathbf{a}, \; . \; . \; . \; ; \qquad (303.)$$

and we may still call the ratio 1 the *zero-power*, and the ratios a, $a \times a$, ... the *positive powers* of the ratio a, even when we cannot continue this series of proportional steps (303.) backward, like the series (259.), so as to determine any contra-positive powers of a; namely, in that particular case when $a = 0$. We may, therefore, consider the equation (264.), $a^0 = 1$, as including even this particular case $a = 0$; and may write

$$0^0 = 1, \qquad (304.)$$

and, therefore, by (301.) and (295.)

$$0^{\frac{0}{m}} = 1: \qquad (305.)$$

we are also conducted to consider the symbols

$$0^{\ominus m}, \quad 0^{\frac{\ominus n}{m}}, \qquad (306.)$$

as absurd, the ratio 0 having no contra-positive powers.

From the generality which we have been led to attribute to the equation $a^0 = 1$, it follows that the symbol

$$1^{\frac{1}{0}}, \text{ and more generally } 1^{\frac{\nu}{0}}, \qquad (307.)$$

is indeterminate, or that it is equally fit to denote all ratios whatever; but that the symbol

$$b^{\frac{1}{0}}, \text{ or } b^{\frac{\nu}{0}}, \text{ if } b \neq 1, \qquad (308.)$$

is absurd, or that it cannot properly denote any ratio. In particular, the symbols

$$0^{\frac{1}{0}}, \quad 0^{\frac{\nu}{0}}, \qquad (309.)$$

are absurd, or denote no ratios whatever. In like manner the symbol

$$0^{\frac{1}{\ominus m}}, \text{ and more generally } 0^{\frac{\nu}{\ominus m}}, \qquad (310.)$$

is absurd, or denotes no ratio, because no ratio a can satisfy the equation

$$a^{\ominus m} = 0. \qquad (311.)$$

We have thus discussed all the nine cases (298.), of powers in which the base is 0, and have found them all to be impossible, except the two first, in which the exponents are $\frac{n}{m}$, and $\frac{0}{m}$, and in which the resulting powers are respectively 0 and 1. We have also obtained sufficient elements for discussing all the other cases (297.) and (299.), with their sub-divisions (300.), as follows.

1st. $\mathrm{B}^{\frac{n}{m}}$ is determined and positive, unless m is even, and n odd; in which case it becomes of the form $\mathrm{B}^{\frac{\ominus 1+2k}{2i}}$, and is ambiguous, being capable of denoting either of two opposite ratios, a positive or a contra-positive. To distinguish these among themselves, we may denote the positive one by the symbol

$$\underset{\circ}{\mathrm{B}}^{\frac{\ominus 1+2k}{2i}}, \qquad (312.)$$

and the contra-positive one by the symbol

$$\Theta\, \underset{\circ}{\mathrm{B}}^{\frac{\ominus 1+2k}{2i}}; \qquad (313.)$$

for example, the two values of the square-root $\sqrt[2]{\mathrm{B}}$ or $\mathrm{B}^{\frac{1}{2}}$, may be denoted for distinction by the two separate symbols

$$\underset{\circ}{\mathrm{B}}^{\frac{1}{2}} = \sqrt{\mathrm{B}}, \quad \Theta\, \underset{\circ}{\mathrm{B}}^{\frac{1}{2}} = \Theta \sqrt{\mathrm{B}}. \qquad (314.)$$

The other three cases of the notation $\mathrm{B}^{\frac{n}{m}}$, namely, the symbols

$$\mathrm{B}^{\frac{\ominus 1+2k}{\ominus 1+2i}}, \quad \mathrm{B}^{\frac{2k}{\ominus 1+2i}}, \quad \mathrm{B}^{\frac{2k}{2i}}, \qquad (315.)$$

denote determined positive ratios.

2d. The three cases

$$\mathrm{B}^{\frac{1+\ominus(2k)}{\ominus 1+2i}}, \quad \mathrm{B}^{\frac{\ominus(2k)}{\ominus 1+2i}}, \quad \mathrm{B}^{\frac{\ominus(2k)}{2i}}, \qquad (316.)$$

of the notation $\mathrm{B}^{\frac{\ominus n}{m}}$, are symbols of determined positive ratios; but the case

$\mathrm{B}^{\frac{1+\Theta(2k)}{2i}}$ is ambiguous, this symbol denoting either a determined positive ratio or a determined contra-positive ratio, which may be thus respectively marked, when we wish to distinguish them from each other,

$$\underset{\circ}{\mathrm{B}}^{\frac{1+\Theta(2k)}{2i}}, \quad \Theta\, \underset{\circ}{\mathrm{B}}^{\frac{1+\Theta(2k)}{2i}}. \qquad (317.)$$

In general, we may write,

$$\mathrm{B}^{\frac{\Theta n}{m}} = \mathfrak{U}\,(\mathrm{B}^{\frac{n}{m}}), \qquad (318.)$$

the latter of these two symbols having the same meaning or meanings as the former.

3d. The symbols

$$\mathrm{B}^{\frac{\Theta 1+2k}{1+\Theta(2i)}}, \quad \mathrm{B}^{\frac{2k}{1+\Theta(2i)}}, \quad \mathrm{B}^{\frac{2k}{\Theta(2i)}}, \qquad (319.)$$

included in the form $\mathrm{B}^{\frac{n}{\Theta m}}$, denote determined positive ratios; but the other symbol $\mathrm{B}^{\frac{\Theta 1+2k}{\Theta(2i)}}$, included in the same form $\mathrm{B}^{\frac{n'}{\Theta m}}$, is ambiguous, denoting either a determined positive or a determined contra-positive ratio,

$$\underset{\circ}{\mathrm{B}}^{\frac{\Theta 1+2k}{\Theta(2i)}}, \text{ or } \Theta\, \underset{\circ}{\mathrm{B}}^{\frac{\Theta 1+2k}{\Theta(2i)}}. \qquad (320.)$$

In general, we may write

$$\mathrm{B}^{\frac{n}{\Theta m}} = \mathfrak{U}\,(\mathrm{B}^{\frac{n}{m}}). \qquad (321.)$$

4th. In like manner, we may write,

$$\mathrm{B}^{\frac{\Theta n}{\Theta m}} = \mathrm{B}^{\frac{n}{m}}, \qquad (322.)$$

the former symbol having always the same meaning or meanings as the latter. The cases

$$\mathrm{B}^{\frac{1+\Theta(2k)}{1+\Theta(2i)}}, \quad \mathrm{B}^{\frac{\Theta(2k)}{1+\Theta(2i)}}, \quad \mathrm{B}^{\frac{\Theta(2k)}{\Theta(2i)}}, \qquad (323.)$$

are symbols of determined positive ratios; but the case $\mathrm{B}^{\frac{1+\Theta 2k)}{\Theta(2i)}}$ is ambiguous, and includes two opposite ratios, which may be thus respectively denoted,

$$\underset{\circ}{\mathrm{B}}^{\frac{1+\Theta(2k)}{\Theta(2i)}}, \quad \Theta\, \underset{\circ}{\mathrm{B}}^{\frac{1+\Theta(2k)}{\Theta(2i)}}. \qquad (324.)$$

In general, we shall denote by the symbol

$$\underset{\circ}{\mathrm{B}}^{\frac{\nu}{\mu}}, \text{ or } \underset{\circ}{b}^{\frac{\nu}{\mu}}, \text{ if } b > 0,\ \mu \neq 0,\ \nu \neq 0, \qquad (325.)$$

that positive ratio which is either the only value, or at least one of the values of the symbol $\mathrm{B}^{\frac{\nu}{\mu}}$ or $b^{\frac{\nu}{\mu}}$; and it is important to observe that this positive ratio is not changed, when the form of the fractional logarithm $\frac{\nu}{\mu}$ is changed, as if it were a fractional multiplier, by the rule (135.), to the form $\frac{\omega \times \nu}{\omega \times \mu}$, or (as it may be more concisely written) $\frac{\omega \nu}{\omega \mu}$; that is,

$$\underset{\circ}{\mathrm{B}}^{\frac{\omega \nu}{\omega \mu}} = \underset{\circ}{\mathrm{B}}^{\frac{\nu}{\mu}} : \qquad (326.)$$

a theorem which is easily proved by means of the relation (268.), combined with the determinateness (already proved) of that positive ratio which results from powering or rooting any proposed positive ratio by any positive or contra-positive whole number.

5th. With respect to the five remaining notations of the group (297.), namely, those in which 0 occurs, we have

$$\mathrm{B}^{\frac{0}{m}} = 1; \quad \mathrm{B}^{\frac{0}{\theta m}} = 1; \qquad (327.)$$

also the symbols

$$\mathrm{B}^{\frac{n}{0}}, \quad \mathrm{B}^{\frac{\theta n}{0}}, \qquad (328.)$$

are each indeterminate when $\mathrm{B} = 1$, and absurd in the contrary case; and, finally, the symbol

$$\mathrm{B}^{\frac{0}{0}} \qquad (329.)$$

is absurd when $\mathrm{B} \neq 1$, but determined and $= 1$, when $\mathrm{B} = 1$.

6th. Proceeding to the group (299.), the symbols

$$(\theta\,\mathrm{B})^{\frac{n}{0}}, \quad (\theta\,\mathrm{B})^{\frac{0}{0}}, \quad (\theta\,\mathrm{B})^{\frac{\theta n}{0}}, \qquad (330.)$$

are absurd; the symbols

$$(\theta\,\mathrm{B})^{\frac{0}{m}}, \quad (\theta\,\mathrm{B})^{\frac{0}{\theta m}}, \qquad (331.)$$

are determined and each $= 1$, if m be odd, but otherwise they are absurd; and the four remaining symbols

$$(\theta\,\mathrm{B})^{\frac{n}{m}}, \quad (\theta\,\mathrm{B})^{\frac{\theta n}{m}}, \quad (\theta\,\mathrm{B})^{\frac{n}{\theta m}}, \quad (\theta\,\mathrm{B})^{\frac{\theta n}{\theta m}}, \qquad (332.)$$

are absurd if m be even, but denote determined ratios when m is odd, which ratios are positive if n be even, but contra-positive if n be odd.

It must be remembered that all the foregoing discussion of the cases of the general notation $b^{\frac{\nu}{\mu}}$, for powers with *fractional* logarithms, is founded on the definition laid down in the 30th article, that $b^{\frac{\nu}{\mu}}$ denotes the ν'th power of a μ'th root of b, or in other words, the ν'th power of a ratio a of which b is the μ'th power. When no such ratio a can be found, consistently with the previous conception of powers with *integer* logarithms, the symbol $b^{\frac{\nu}{\mu}}$ is pronounced to be *absurd*, or to be incapable of denoting any ratio consistently with its general definition; and when two or more such ratios a can be found, each having its μ'th power $= b$, we have pronounced that the fractional power $b^{\frac{\nu}{\mu}}$ is *ambiguous* or *indeterminate*, except in those cases in which the second component act of powering by the numerator ν has happened to destroy the indeterminateness. And with respect to powers with *integer* exponents, it is to be remembered that we always define them by a reference to a series of proportional steps, of which at least the original step (corresponding to the zero-power) is supposed to be an *effective* step, and which can always be continued indefinitely, at least in the positive direction, that is, in the way of *repeated multiplication* by the ratio proposed as the base, although in the particular case of a null ratio, we cannot continue the series backward by *division*, so as to find any contra-positive powers. These definitions appear to be the most natural; but others might have been assumed, and then other results would have followed. In general, the definitions of mathematical science are not altogether arbitrary, but a certain discretion is allowed in the selection of them, although when once selected, they must then be consistently reasoned from.

33. The foregoing article enables us to assign one determined positive ratio, and only one, as denoted by the symbol $\underset{\circ}{b}^{a}$, when b is any determined positive ratio, and a any fractional number with a numerator and a denominator each different from 0: it shows also that this ratio $\underset{\circ}{b}^{a}$ does not change when we transform the expression of the fractional logarithm a by introducing or suppressing any whole number ω as a factor common to both numerator and denominator; and permits us to write

$$\underset{\circ}{b}^{\ominus a} = \text{ꓤ}\,(\underset{\circ}{b}^{a}), \qquad (333.)$$

$\ominus a$ being the opposite of the fraction a in the sense of the 17th article. More generally, by the meaning of the notation $\underset{\circ}{b}^{a}$, and by the determinateness of those positive ratios which result from the powering or rooting of determined positive ratios by determined integer numbers, (setting aside the impossible or indeterminate case of rooting by the number 0,) we have the relation

$$\underset{\circ}{b}^{\beta} \times \underset{\circ}{b}^{\alpha} = \underset{\circ}{b}^{\beta+\alpha}, \qquad (334.)$$

which is analogous to (267.); and the relation

$$\underset{\circ}{c}^{\beta} = \underset{\circ}{b}^{\beta\times\alpha} \text{ if } c = \underset{\circ}{b}^{\alpha}, \qquad (335.)$$

analogous to (268.): α and β denoting here any two commensurable numbers. And it is easy to see that while the fractional exponent or logarithm α increases, advancing successively through all fractional states in the progression from contra-positive to positive, the positive ratio $\underset{\circ}{b}^{\alpha}$ increases constantly if $b > 1$, or else decreases constantly if $b < 1$, $(b > 0,)$ or remains constantly $= 1$ if $b = 1$. But to show that this increase or decrease of the power with the exponent is *continuous* as well as constant, we must establish principles for the interpretation of the symbol $\underset{\circ}{b}^{\alpha}$ when α is not a fraction.

When α is incommensurable, but b still positive, it may be proved that we shall still have these last relations (334.) and (335.), if we interpret the symbol $\underset{\circ}{b}^{\alpha}$ to denote that determined positive ratio c which satisfies the following conditions:

$$\left.\begin{aligned} c = \underset{\circ}{b}^{\alpha} > \underset{\circ}{b}^{\frac{n'}{m'}} &\text{ whenever } \alpha > \tfrac{n'}{m'}, \\ c = \underset{\circ}{b}^{\alpha} < \underset{\circ}{b}^{\frac{n''}{m''}} &\text{ whenever } \alpha < \tfrac{n''}{m''}, \\ &\text{if } b > 1; \end{aligned}\right\} \qquad (336.)$$

or else these other conditions,

$$\left.\begin{aligned} c = \underset{\circ}{b}^{\alpha} < \underset{\circ}{b}^{\frac{n'}{m'}} &\text{ whenever } \alpha > \tfrac{n'}{m'}, \\ c = \underset{\circ}{b}^{\alpha} > \underset{\circ}{b}^{\frac{n''}{m''}} &\text{ whenever } \alpha < \tfrac{n''}{m''}, \\ &\text{if } b < 1,\ b > 0; \end{aligned}\right\} \qquad (337.)$$

or finally this equation,

$$c = \underset{\circ}{b}^{\alpha} = 1, \text{ if } b = 1. \qquad (338.)$$

The reader will soon perceive the reasonableness of these interpretations; but he may desire to see it proved that the conditions (336.) or (337.) can always be satisfied by one positive ratio c, and only one, whatever determined ratio may be denoted by α, and whatever positive ratio (different from 1) by b. That *at least one* such positive ratio $c = \underset{\circ}{b}^{a}$ can be found, whatever incommensurable number the exponent a may be, is easily proved from the circumstance that none of the conditions (336.) are incompatible with one another if $b > 1$, and that none of the conditions (337.) are incompatible with each other in the contrary case, by reason of the constant increase or constant decrease of the fractional power $\underset{\circ}{b}^{\frac{n}{m}}$ for constantly increasing values of the fractional exponent $\frac{n}{m}$. And that *only one* such positive ratio $c = \underset{\circ}{b}^{a}$ can be found, or that no two different positive ratios c, c', can *both* satisfy *all* these conditions may be proved for the case $b > 1$ by the following process, which can without difficulty be adapted to the other case.

The fractional powers of b comprised in the series

$$\underset{\circ}{b}^{\frac{1}{m}}, \underset{\circ}{b}^{\frac{2}{m}}, \underset{\circ}{b}^{\frac{3}{m}}, \ldots \underset{\circ}{b}^{\frac{im}{m}}, \underset{\circ}{b}^{\frac{1+im}{m}}, \qquad (339.)$$

increase (when $b > 1$) by increasing differences, of which the last is

$$\Theta\, \underset{\circ}{b}^{\frac{im}{m}} + \underset{\circ}{b}^{\frac{1+im}{m}} = b^{i}\,(\Theta\, 1 + \underset{\circ}{b}^{\frac{1}{m}}); \qquad (340.)$$

this last difference, therefore, and by still stronger reason each of the others which precede it, will be less than $\frac{1}{k}$, if

$$l > k\, b^{i} \qquad (341.)$$

and

$$\Theta\, 1 + \underset{\circ}{b}^{\frac{1}{m}} < \frac{1}{l}: \qquad (342.)$$

and this last condition will be satisfied, if

$$m > l\,(\Theta\, 1 + b), \qquad (343.)$$

l and m (like i and k) denoting any positive whole numbers; for then we shall have

$$1 + \frac{m}{l} > b, \qquad (344.)$$

and by still stronger reason

$$\left(1 \times \frac{1}{l}\right)^{m} > b,\ 1 + \frac{1}{l} > \underset{\circ}{b}^{\frac{1}{m}}, \qquad (345.)$$

observing that

$$\left(1 + \frac{1}{l}\right)^{m} > 1 + \frac{m}{l},\ \text{if } m > 1, \qquad (346.)$$

because, by the theorem of multiplication (273.), or (281.),

$$\Theta 1 + \left(1 + \frac{1}{l}\right)^{m} = \frac{1}{l} \left\{ 1 + \left(1 + \frac{1}{l}\right) + \left(1 + \frac{1}{l}\right)^{2} + \dots + \left(1 + \frac{1}{l}\right)^{\Theta 1 + m} \right\}. \quad (347.)$$

If then $c\ c'$ be any two proposed unequal positive ratios, of which we may suppose that c' is the greater,

$$c' > c, \ c > 0, \quad (348.)$$

we may choose two positive whole numbers i, k, so large that

$$b^{i} > c', \ \frac{1}{k} < \Theta c + c', \quad (349.)$$

and two other positive whole numbers l, m, large enough to satisfy the conditions (341.) (343.); and then we shall be sure that some one at least, such as $\underset{0}{b}^{\frac{n}{m}}$, of the fractional powers of b comprised in the series (339.) will fall between the two proposed unequal ratios $c\ c'$, so that

$$c < \underset{0}{b}^{\frac{n}{m}}, \ c' > \underset{0}{b}^{\frac{n}{m}}. \quad (350.)$$

If then the one ratio c satisfy all the conditions (336.), the incommensurable number a must be $< \frac{n}{m}$, and therefore, by the 2nd relation (350.), the other ratio c' cannot also satisfy all the conditions of the same form, since it is $> \underset{0}{b}^{\frac{n}{m}}$, although $a < \frac{n}{m}$. In like manner, if the greater ratio c' satisfy all the conditions of the form (336.) the lesser ratio c cannot also satisfy them all, because in this case the incommensurable number a will be $> \frac{n}{m}$. No two unequal positive ratios, therefore, can satisfy all those conditions: they are therefore satisfied by one positive ratio and only one, and the symbol $\underset{\bullet}{b}^{a}$ (interpreted by them) denotes a determined positive ratio when $b > 1$. For a similar reason the same symbol $\underset{0}{b}^{a}$, interpreted by the conditions (337.), denotes a determined positive ratio when $b < 1$, $b > 0$; and for the remaining case of a positive base, $b = 1$, the symbol $\underset{\bullet}{b}^{a}$ denotes still, by (338.) a determined positive ratio, namely, the ratio 1. The exponent or logarithm a has, in these late investigations, been supposed to be incommensurable; when that exponent a is commensurable, the base b being still positive, we saw that the symbol $\underset{0}{b}^{a}$ can be interpreted more easily, as a power of a root, and that it always denotes a determined positive ratio.

Reciprocally, in the equation

$$c = \underset{\bullet}{b}^{a}, \quad (351.)$$

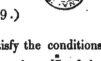

if the power c be any determined positive ratio, and if the exponent a be any determined ratio, positive or contra-positive, we can deduce the positive base or ratio b, by calculating the inverse or reciprocal power

$$b = \underset{\circ}{c}^{\,1\,a}; \qquad (352.)$$

as appears from the relation (335.) which extends, as was above announced, together with the relation (334.), even to the case of incommensurable exponents. The proof of the important extension last alluded to, will easily suggest itself to those who have studied the foregoing demonstrations; and they will perceive that with the foregoing rules for the interpretation of the symbol $\underset{\circ}{b}^{a}$, for the case of an incommensurable exponent, the power $\underset{\circ}{b}^{a}$ increases (as was said above) *continuously* as well as *constantly* with the exponent a if the base b be > 1, or else decreases continuously and constantly if that positive base be < 1, but remains constantly $= 1$ if $b = 1$. It is therefore possible to find one determined exponent or logarithm a, and only one, which shall satisfy the equation (351.), when the power c and the base b are any given positive ratios, except in the impossible or indeterminate case when this base b is the particular ratio 1; and the number a thus determined, whether positive or contra-positive or null, may be called "the logarithm of c to the base b," and may be denoted by the symbol

$$a = \log_{b} . \, c. \qquad (353.)$$

It is still more easy to perceive, finally, that when this logarithm a is given, (even if it be incommensurable,) the power c increases constantly and continuously from zero with the base b, if $a > 0$, or else decreases constantly and continuously towards zero if $a < 0$, or remains constant and $= 1$, if $a = 0$.

Remarks on the Notation of this Essay, and on some modifications by which it may be made more like the Notation commonly employed.

34. In the foregoing articles we have constantly denoted *moments*, or indivisible points of time, by small capital letters, A, B, A′, B′, &c.; and *steps*, or transitions from one such moment to others, by small Roman letters, a, b, a′, b′, &c. The mark − has been interposed between the marks of two moments, to express the ordinal relation of those two moments, or the step which must be made in order to pass from one to the other; and the mark + has been inserted between the marks of a step and a moment, or between the marks of two steps, to denote the application of the

step to the moment, or the composition of the two steps with each other. For the decomposition of a step into others, we have used no special mark; but employed the theorem that such decomposition can be performed by compounding with the given compound step the opposites of the given component steps, and a special notation for such opposite steps, namely, the mark* Θ prefixed; so that we have written Θ a to denote the step opposite to the step a, and consequently Θ a + b to denote the algebraical excess of the step b over the step a, because this excess may be conceived as a step compounded of b and Θ a. However, we might have agreed to write

$$(\mathrm{b}+\mathrm{A})-(\mathrm{a}+\mathrm{A})=\mathrm{b}-\mathrm{a}, \qquad (354.)$$

denoting the step from the moment a + A to the moment b + A, for conciseness by b − a; and then b − a would have been another symbol for the algebraical excess of the step b over the step a, and we should have had the equation

$$\mathrm{b}-\mathrm{a}=\Theta\,\mathrm{a}+\mathrm{b}. \qquad (355.)$$

We might thus have been led to interpose the mark − between the marks of a compound step b and a component step a, in order to denote the other component step, or the algebraical *remainder* which results from the algebraical *subtraction* of the component from the compound.

Again, we have used the Greek letters μ ν ξ ρ ω, with or without accents, to denote *integer numbers* in general, and the italic letters *i k l m n* to denote positive whole numbers in particular; using also the earlier letters α β γ *a b c d* to denote any ratios whatever, commensurable or incommensurable, and in one recent investigation the capital letter B to denote any positive ratio; and employed, in the combination of these symbols of numbers, or of ratios, the same marks of *addition* and of *opposition*, + and Θ, which had been already employed for steps, and the mark of multiplication ×, without any special mark for *subtraction*. We might, however, have agreed to write, in general,

$$(b\times\mathrm{a})-(a\times\mathrm{a})=(b-a)\times\mathrm{a}, \qquad (356.)$$

as we wrote

$$(b\times\mathrm{a})+(a\times\mathrm{a})=(b+a)\times\mathrm{a};$$

and then the symbol $b-a$ would have denoted the algebraical excess of the number

* This mark has been printed, for want of the proper type, like a Greek Theta in this Essay: it was designed to be printed thus $\ominus$.

b over the number a, or the remainder obtained by the algebraical *subtraction* of the latter number from the former; and we should have had the equation,

$$b-a=\Theta\, a+b, \qquad (357.)$$

which is, with respect to *numbers*, or ratios, what the equation (355.) is, with respect to steps. And when such symbols of remainders, $\mathrm{b}-\mathrm{a}$ or $b-a$, are to be combined with other symbols in the way of algebraical *addition*, it results, from principles already explained, that they need not be enclosed in parentheses; for example, we may write simply $\mathrm{c}+\mathrm{b}-\mathrm{a}$ instead of $\mathrm{c}+(\mathrm{b}-\mathrm{a})$, because the sum denoted by this last notation is equivalent to the remainder $(\mathrm{c}+\mathrm{b})-\mathrm{a}$. But the parentheses (or some other combining mark) must be used, when a remainder is to be *subtracted;* thus the symbol $\mathrm{c}-\mathrm{b}-\mathrm{a}$ is to be interpreted as $(\mathrm{c}-\mathrm{b})-\mathrm{a}$, and not as $\mathrm{c}-(\mathrm{b}-\mathrm{a})$, which latter symbol is equivalent to $(\mathrm{c}-\mathrm{b})+\mathrm{a}$, or $\mathrm{c}-\mathrm{b}+\mathrm{a}$.

35. With this way of denoting the algebraical subtraction of steps, and that of numbers, we have the formulæ

$$0-\mathrm{a}=\Theta\,\mathrm{a}, \quad 0-a=\Theta\, a, \qquad (358.)$$

0 denoting in the one a null step, and in the other a null number. And if we farther agree to suppress (for abridgement) this symbol 0 when it occurs in such combinations as the following, $0+\mathrm{a}$, $0-\mathrm{a}$, $0+a$, $0-a$, writing, in the case of steps,

$$0+\mathrm{a}=+\mathrm{a}, \quad 0-\mathrm{a}=-\mathrm{a}, \qquad (359.)$$

and similarly, in the case of numbers,

$$0+a=+a, \quad 0-a=-a, \qquad (360.)$$

and, in like manner,

$$\left.\begin{array}{l} 0+\mathrm{a}\pm\mathrm{b}=+\mathrm{a}\pm\mathrm{b}, \quad 0-\mathrm{a}\pm\mathrm{b}=-\mathrm{a}\pm\mathrm{b}, \\ 0+a\pm b=+a\pm b, \quad 0-a\pm b=-a\pm b, \end{array}\right\} \qquad (361.)$$

we shall then have the formulæ

$$+\mathrm{a}=\mathrm{a}, \quad -\mathrm{a}=\Theta\,\mathrm{a}, \qquad (362.)$$

and

$$+a=a, \quad -a=\Theta\, a, \qquad (363.)$$

of which the one refers to steps and the other to numbers. With these conventions, the prefixing of the mark + to an isolated symbol of a step or of a number, does not change the meaning of the symbol; but the prefixing of the mark − converts that symbol into another, which denotes the opposite of the original step, or the opposite of the original number; so that the series of whole numbers (103.) or (266.) may be written as follows:

$$\ldots\ -3,\ -2,\ -1,\ 0,\ +1,\ +2,\ +3,\ \ldots \qquad (364.)$$

Also, in this notation,

$$\left.\begin{array}{l} \mathrm{b} \pm (+\mathrm{a}) = \mathrm{b} \pm \mathrm{a},\ \mathrm{b} \pm (-\mathrm{a}) = \mathrm{b} \mp \mathrm{a}, \\ b \pm (+a) = b \pm a,\ b \pm (-a) = b \mp a. \end{array}\right\} \qquad (365.)$$

36. Finally, as we wrote, for the case of commensurable steps,

$$\frac{\nu \times \mathrm{a}}{\mu \times \mathrm{a}} = \frac{\nu}{\mu},$$

μ and ν being here whole numbers, so we may agree to write, in general,

$$\frac{b \times \mathrm{a}}{a \times \mathrm{a}} = \frac{b}{a}, \qquad (366.)$$

whatever ratios a and b may be; and then this symbol $\frac{b}{a}$ will denote, in general, the algebraic quotient obtained by dividing the number or ratio b by the number or ratio a; whereas we had before no general way of denoting such a quotient, except by the mark ꓤ prefixed to the symbol of the divisor a, so as to form a symbol of the reciprocal number ꓤ a, to multiply by which latter number is equivalent to dividing by the former. Comparing the two notations, we have the formula,

$$\frac{1}{a} = \text{ꓤ}\, a, \qquad (367.)$$

and generally

$$\frac{b}{a} = \text{ꓤ}\, a \times b = b \times \text{ꓤ}\, a. \qquad (368.)$$

These two marks Θ and ꓤ have been the only *new* marks introduced in this Elementary Essay; although the notation employed for powers differs a little from the common notation: especially the symbol $\overset{}{\underset{\circ}{b}}{}^{a}$, suggested by those researches of Mr. Graves respecting the general expression of powers and logarithms, which were the first occasion of the conception of that Theory of Conjugate Functions to which we now proceed.

END OF THE PRELIMINARY AND ELEMENTARY ESSAY.

THEORY OF CONJUGATE FUNCTIONS,

OR ALGEBRAIC COUPLES.

On Couples of Moments, and of Steps, in Time.

1. When we have imagined any one moment of time A_1, which we may call a *primary moment*, we may again imagine a moment of time A_2, and may call this a *secondary moment*, without regarding whether it follows, or coincides with, or precedes the primary, in the common progression of time; we may also speak of this primary and this secondary moment as forming a *couple of moments*, or a *moment-couple*, which may be denoted thus, (A_1, A_2). Again, we may imagine any other two moments, a primary and a secondary, B_1 and B_2, distinct from or coincident with each other, and forming another *moment-couple*, (B_1, B_2); and we may compare the latter couple of moments with the former, moment with moment, primary with primary, and secondary with secondary, examining how B_1 is ordinally related to A_1, and how B_2 is ordinally related to A_2, in the progression of time, as coincident, or subsequent, or precedent; and thus may obtain a *couple of ordinal relations*, which may be thus separately denoted $B_1 - A_1$, $B_2 - A_2$, or thus collectively, as a *relation-couple*,

$$(B_1 - A_1, \; B_2 - A_2).$$

This couple of ordinal relations between moments may also be conceived as constituting a complex *relation of one moment-couple to another*; and in conformity with this conception it may be thus denoted,

$$(B_1, B_2) - (A_1, A_2),$$

so that, comparing this with the former way of representing it, we may establish the written equation,

$$(B_1, B_2) - (A_1, A_2) = (B_1 - A_1, B_2 - A_2). \qquad (1.)$$

Instead of conceiving thus a couple of ordinal relations between moments, or a relation between two couples of moments, discovered by the (analytic) *comparison* of one such couple of moments with another, we may conceive a *couple of steps* in the progression of time, from moment to moment respectively, or a single complex step which we may call a *step-couple* from one moment-couple to another, serving to *generate* (synthetically) one of these moment-couples from the other; and if we denote the two separate steps by a_1, a_2, (a_1 being the step from A_1 to B_1, and a_2 being the step from A_2 to B_2,) so that in the notation of the Preliminary Essay,

$$B_1 = a_1 + A_1, \quad B_2 = a_2 + A_2,$$
$$B_1 = (B_1 - A_1) + A_1, \quad B_2 = (B_2 - A_2) + A_2,$$

we may now establish this analogous notation for couples,

$$\left.\begin{aligned}(B_1, B_2) &= (a_1 + A_1, \; a_2' + A_2) \\ &= (a_1, a_2) + (A_1, A_2) \\ &= \{(B_1, B_2) - (A_1, A_2)\} + (A_1, A_2),\end{aligned}\right\} \qquad (2.)$$

the symbol $(B_1, B_2) - (A_1, A_2)$ corresponding now to the conception of the *step-couple* by which we may pass from the *moment-couple* (A_1, A_2) to the *moment-couple* (B_1, B_2), and the equivalent symbol (a_1, a_2) or $(B_1 - A_1, B_2 - A_2)$ corresponding now to the conception of the *couple of steps* a_1, a_2, from the two moments A_1, A_2, to the two moments B_1, B_2, respectively. The step a_1, or $B_1 - A_1$ may be called the *primary step* of the couple (a_1, a_2), and the step a_2 or $B_2 - A_2$ may be called the *secondary step*.

A step-couple may be said to be *effective* when it actually changes the moment-couple to which it is applied; that is, when one at least of its two coupled steps is effective: and in the contrary case, that is, when both those coupled steps are separately null, the step-couple itself may be said to be *null* also. And effective step-couples may be distinguished into *singly effective* and *doubly effective* step-couples, according as they alter *one* or *both* of the two moments of the moment-couples to which they are applied. Finally, a singly effective step-couple may be called a *pure primary* or *pure secondary* step-couple, according as only its primary or only its secondary step is effective, that is, according as it alters only the primary or only the secondary moment. Thus (0, 0) is a null step-couple, (a_1, a_2) is a doubly effective step-couple, and $(a_1, 0)$ $(0, a_2)$ are singly effective step-couples, the former $(a_1, 0)$ being a pure primary, and the latter $(0, a_2)$ being a pure secondary, if 0 denote a null step, and a_1 a_2 effective steps.

On the Composition and Decomposition of Step-Couples.

2. Having stepped from one couple of moments (A_1, A_2) to another couple of moments (B_1, B_2) by one step-couple (a_1, a_2), we may afterwards step to a third couple of moments (C_1, C_2) by a second step-couple (b_1, b_2), so as to have

$$\left.\begin{aligned}(C_1, C_2) &= (b_1, b_2) + (B_1, B_2),\\ (B_1, B_2) &= (a_1, a_2) + (A_1, A_2);\end{aligned}\right\} \quad (3.)$$

and then we may consider ourselves as having made upon the whole a compound couple of steps, or a *compound step-couple*, from the first moment-couple (A_1, A_2) to the third moment-couple (C_1, C_2), and may agree to call this compound step-couple the *sum* of the two component step-couples (a_1, a_2), (b_1, b_2), or to say that is formed by *adding* them, and to denote as follows,

$$(C_1, C_2) - (A_1, A_2) = (b_1, b_2) + (a_1, a_2); \quad (4.)$$

as, in the language of the Preliminary Essay, the two separate compound steps, from A_1 to C_1 and from A_2 to C_2 are the *sums* of the component steps, and are denoted by the symbols $b_1 + a_1$ and $b_2 + a_2$ respectively. With these notations, we have evidently the equation

$$(b_1, b_2) + (a_1, a_2) = (b_1 + a_1, b_2 + a_2); \quad (5.)$$

that is, the *sum of two step-couples may be formed by coupling the two sum-steps.* Hence, also,

$$(b_1, b_2) + (a_1, a_2) = (a_1, a_2) + (b_1, b_2), \quad (6.)$$

that is, *the order of any two component step-couples may be changed without altering the result;* and

$$(a_1, a_2) = (a_1, 0) + (0, a_2), \quad (7.)$$

that is, *every doubly effective step-couple is the sum of a pure primary and a pure secondary*. In like manner, we can conceive sums of more than two step-couples, and may establish, for such sums, relations analogous to those marked (5.) and (6.); thus,

$$\left.\begin{aligned}(c_1, c_2)+(b_1, b_2)+(a_1, a_2)&=(c_1+b_1+a_1, c_2+b_2+a_2),\\ &=(a_1, a_2)+(b_1, b_2)+(c_1, c_2) \text{ \&c.}\end{aligned}\right\} \quad (8.)$$

We may also consider the *decomposition* of a step-couple, or the *subtraction* of one such step-couple from another, and may write,

$$(b_1, b_2)-(a_1, a_2)=(b_1-a_1, b_2-a_2), \quad (9.)$$

$(b_1, b_2)-(a_1, a_2)$ being that sought step-couple which must be compounded with or added to the given component step-couple (a_1, a_2) in order to produce the given compound step-couple (b_1, b_2). And if we agree to suppress the symbol of a null step-couple, when it is combined with others or others with it in the way of addition or subtraction, we may write

$$\left.\begin{aligned}(a_1, a_2)&=(0, 0)+(a_1, a_2)=+(a_1, a_2),\\ (-a_1, -a_2)&=(0, 0)-(a_1, a_2)=-(a_1, a_2),\end{aligned}\right\} \quad (10.)$$

employing a notation analogous to that explained for single steps in the 35th article of the Preliminary Essay. Thus $+(a_1, a_2)$ is another way of denoting the step-couple (a_1, a_2) itself; and $-(a_1, a_2)$ is a way of denoting the *opposite* step-couple $(-a_1, -a_2)$.

On the Multiplication of a Step-Couple by a Number.

3. From any proposed moment-couple (A_1, A_2), and any proposed step-couple (a_1, a_2), we may generate a series of other moment-couples

$$\ldots (E'_1, E'_2), (E_1, E_2), (A_1, A_2), (B_1, B_2), (B'_1, B'_2) \ldots \quad (11.)$$

by repeatedly applying this step-couple (a_1, a_2), itself, and the opposite step-couple $-(a_1, a_2)$, or $(-a_1, -a_2)$, in a way analogous to the process of the 13th article of the Preliminary Essay, as follows:

$$\left.\begin{aligned}
&\ldots\ldots\ldots\ldots \\
(E'_1, E'_2) &= (-a_1, -a_2) + (-a_1, -a_2) + (A_1, A_2), \\
(E_1, E_2) &= (-a_1, -a_2) + (A_1, A_1), \\
(A_1, A_2) &= (A_1, A_2), \\
(B_1, B_2) &= (a_1, a_2) + (A_1, A_2), \\
(B'_1, B'_2) &= (a_1, a_2) + (a\ , a_2) + (A_1, A_2), \\
&\ldots\ldots\ldots\ldots
\end{aligned}\right\} \qquad (12.)$$

and a series of *multiple step-couples*, namely

$$\left.\begin{aligned}
&\ldots\ldots\ldots\ldots \\
(E'_1, E'_2) - (A_1, A_2) &= (-a_1, -a_2) + (-a_1, -a_2), \\
(E_1, E_2) - (A_1, A_2) &= (-a_1, -a_2) \\
(A_1, A_2) - (A_1, A_2) &= (0, 0), \\
(B_1, B_2) - (A_1, A_2) &= (a_1, a_2), \\
(B'_1, B'_2) - (A_1, A_2) &= (a_1, a_2) + (a_1, a_2), \\
&\ldots\ldots\ldots\ldots
\end{aligned}\right\} \qquad (13.)$$

which may be thus more concisely denoted,

$$\left.\begin{aligned}
&\ldots\ldots\ldots\ldots \\
(E'_1, E'_2) &= -2\,(a_1, a_2) + (A_1, A_2), \\
(E_1, E_2) &= -1\,(a_1, a_2) + (A_1, A_2), \\
(A_1, A_2) &= 0\,(a_1, a_2) + (A_1, A_2), \\
(B_1, B_2) &= +1\,(a_1, a_2) + (A_1, A_2), \\
(B'\ , B'_2) &= +2\,(a_1, a_2) + (A_1, A_2), \\
&\ldots\ldots\ldots\ldots
\end{aligned}\right\} \qquad (14.)$$

and

$$\left.\begin{aligned}
&\ldots\ldots\ldots\ldots \\
(E'_1, E'_2) - (A_1, A_2) &= -2\,(a_1, a_2) = -2 \times (a_1, a_2), \\
(E_1, E_2) - (A_1, A_2) &= -1\,(a_1, a_2) = -1 \times (a_1, a_2), \\
(A_1, A_2) - (A_1, A_2) &= 0\,(a_1, a_2) = 0 \times (a_1, a_2), \\
(B_1, B_2) - (A_1, A_2) &= +1\,(a_1, a_2) = +1 \times (a_1, a_2), \\
(B'_1, B'_2) - (A_1, A_2) &= +2\,(a_1, a_2) = +2 \times (a_1, a_2), \\
&\&c.
\end{aligned}\right\} \qquad (15.)$$

We may also conceive step-couples which shall be *sub-multiples* and *fractions* of a given step-couple, and may write

$$(c_1, c_2) = \frac{\nu}{\mu} \times (b_1, b_2) = \frac{\nu}{\mu}(b_1, b_2), \qquad (16.)$$

when the two step-couples $(\mathfrak{b}_1, \mathfrak{b}_2)$ $(\mathfrak{c}_1, \mathfrak{c}_2)$ are related as multiples to one common step-couple $(\mathfrak{a}_1, \mathfrak{a}_2)$ as follows:

$$(\mathfrak{b}_1, \mathfrak{b}_2) = \mu \times (\mathfrak{a}_1, \mathfrak{a}_1), \; (\mathfrak{c}_1, \mathfrak{c}_2) = \nu \times (\mathfrak{a}_1, \mathfrak{a}_2), \qquad (17.)$$

μ and ν boing any two proposed whole numbers. And if we suppose the *fractional multiplier* $\frac{\nu}{\mu}$ in (16.) to tend to any *incommensurable limit* a, we may denote by $a \times (\mathfrak{b}_1, \mathfrak{b}_2)$ the corresponding limit of the fractional product, and may consider this latter limit as the *product* obtained by multiplying the step-couple $(\mathfrak{b}_1, \mathfrak{b}_2)$ by the *incommensurable multiplier* or number a; so that we may write,

$$\left. \begin{array}{l} (\mathfrak{c}_1, \mathfrak{c}_2) = a \times (\mathfrak{b}_1, \mathfrak{b}_2) = a\,(\mathfrak{b}_1, \mathfrak{b}_2), \\ \text{if } (\mathfrak{c}_1, \mathfrak{c}_2) = \underline{\mathrm{L}}\,(\frac{\nu}{\mu}(\mathfrak{b}_1, \mathfrak{b}_2)) \text{ and } a = \underline{\mathrm{L}}\,\frac{\nu}{\mu}, \end{array} \right\} \qquad (18.)$$

using $\underline{\mathrm{L}}$ as the mark of a limit, as in the notation of the Preliminary Essay. It follows from these conceptions of the multiplication of a step-couple by a number, that generally

$$a \times (\mathfrak{a}_1, \mathfrak{a}_2) = (a\,\mathfrak{a}_1, a\,\mathfrak{a}_2), \qquad (19.)$$

whatever steps may be denoted by $\mathfrak{a}_1$, $\mathfrak{a}_2$, and whatever number (commensurable or incommensurable, and positive or contra-positive or null) may be denoted by a. Hence also we may write

$$\frac{(a\,\mathfrak{a}_1, a\,\mathfrak{a}_2)}{(\mathfrak{a}_1, \mathfrak{a}_2)} = a, \qquad (20.)$$

and may consider the number a as expressing the *ratio* of the step-couple $(a\,\mathfrak{a}_1, a\,\mathfrak{a}_2)$ to the step-couple $(\mathfrak{a}_1, \mathfrak{a}_2)$.

On the Multiplication of a Step-Couple by a Number-Couple; and on the Ratio of one Step-Couple to another.

4. The formula (20.) enables us, in an infinite variety of cases, to assign a single number a as the ratio of one proposed step-couple $(\mathfrak{b}_1, \mathfrak{b}_2)$ to another $(\mathfrak{a}_1, \mathfrak{a}_2)$; namely, in all those cases in which the primary and secondary steps of the one couple are proportional to those of the other: but it fails to assign such a ratio, in all those

other cases in which this condition is not satisfied. The spirit of the present Theory of Couples leads us, however, to conceive that the ratio of any one effective step-couple to any other may perhaps be expressed in general by a *number-couple*, or couple of numbers, a primary and a secondary; and that with reference to this more general view of such ratio, the relation (20.) might be more fully written thus,

$$\frac{(a_1 \mathrm{a}_1, a_1 \mathrm{a}_2)}{(\mathrm{a}_1, \mathrm{a}_2)} = (a_1, 0), \qquad (21.)$$

and the relation (19.) as follows,

$$(a_1, 0) \times (\mathrm{a}_1, \mathrm{a}_2) = (a_1, 0)(\mathrm{a}_1, \mathrm{a}_2) = (a_1 \mathrm{a}_1, a_1 \mathrm{a}_2), \qquad (22.)$$

the single number a_1 being changed to the couple $(a_1, 0)$, which may be called a *pure primary number-couple.* The spirit of this theory of primaries and secondaries leads us also to conceive that the ratio of any step-couple $(\mathrm{b}_1, \mathrm{b}_2)$ to any pure primary step-couple $(\mathrm{a}_1, 0)$, may be expressed by coupling the two ratios $\frac{\mathrm{b}_1}{\mathrm{a}_1}, \frac{\mathrm{b}_2}{\mathrm{a}_1}$, which the two steps $\mathrm{b}_1, \mathrm{b}_2$ bear to the effective primary step a_1; so that we may write

$$\frac{(\mathrm{b}_1, \mathrm{b}_2)}{(\mathrm{a}_1, 0)} = \left(\frac{\mathrm{b}_1}{\mathrm{a}_1}, \frac{\mathrm{b}_2}{\mathrm{a}_1}\right), \quad \frac{(a_1 \mathrm{a}_1, a_2 \mathrm{a}_1)}{(\mathrm{a}_1, 0)} = (a_1, a_2), \qquad (23.)$$

and in like manner, by the general connexion of multiplication with ratio,

$$(a_1, a_2) \times (\mathrm{a}_1, 0) = (a_1, a_2)(\mathrm{a}_1, 0) = (a_1 \mathrm{a}_1, a_2 \mathrm{a}_1). \qquad (24.)$$

From the relations (22.) (24.), it follows by (5.) that

$$(b_1 + a_1, 0)(\mathrm{a}_1, \mathrm{a}_2) = (b_1, 0)(\mathrm{a}_1, \mathrm{a}_2) + (a_1, 0)(\mathrm{a}_1, \mathrm{a}_2), \qquad (25.)$$

and that

$$(a_1, a_2)(\mathrm{b}_1 + \mathrm{a}_1, 0) = (a_1, a_2)(\mathrm{b}_1, 0) + (a_1, a_2)(\mathrm{a}_1, 0); \qquad (26.)$$

and the spirit of the present extension of reasonings and operations on single moments, steps, and numbers, to moment-couples, step-couples, and number-couples, leads us to determine (if we can) what remains yet undetermined in the conception of a number-couple, as a multiplier or as a ratio, so as to satisfy the two following more general conditions,

$$(b_1 + a_1, b_2 + a_2)(\mathrm{a}_1, \mathrm{a}_2) = (b_1, b_2)(\mathrm{a}_1, \mathrm{a}_2) + (a_1, a_2)(\mathrm{a}_1, \mathrm{a}_2), \qquad (27.)$$

and

$$(a_1, a_2)(\mathrm{b}_1 + \mathrm{a}_1, \mathrm{b}_2 + \mathrm{a}_2) = (a_1, a_2)(\mathrm{b}_1, \mathrm{b}_2) + (a_1, a_2)(\mathrm{a}_1, \mathrm{a}_2), \qquad (28.)$$

whatever numbers may be denoted by $a_1\ a_2\ b_1\ b_2$, and whatever steps by $\mathfrak{a}_1\ \mathfrak{a}_2\ \mathfrak{b}_1\ \mathfrak{b}_2$. With these conditions we have

$$(a_1, a_2)\ (\mathfrak{a}_1, \mathfrak{a}_2) = (a_1, 0)\ (\mathfrak{a}_1, \mathfrak{a}_2) + (0, a_2)\ (\mathfrak{a}_1, \mathfrak{a}_2), \qquad (29.)$$

$$(0, a_2)\ (\mathfrak{a}_1, \mathfrak{a}_2) = (0, a_2)\ (\mathfrak{a}_1, 0) + (0, a_2)\ (0, \mathfrak{a}_2), \qquad (30.)$$

and, therefore, by (22.) and (24.), and by the formula for sums,

$$(a_1, a_2)\ (\mathfrak{a}_1, \mathfrak{a}_2) = (a_1\,\mathfrak{a}_1,\ a_1\,\mathfrak{a}_2) + (0,\ a_2\,\mathfrak{a}_1) + (0, a_2)\ (0, \mathfrak{a}_2)$$

$$= (a_1\,\mathfrak{a}_1,\ a_1\,\mathfrak{a}_2 + a_2\,\mathfrak{a}_1) + (0, a_2)\ (0, \mathfrak{a}_2), \qquad (31.)$$

in which the product $(0, a_2)\ (0, \mathfrak{a}_2)$ remains still undetermined. It must, however, by the spirit of the present theory, be supposed to be some step-couple,

$$(0, a_2)\ (0, \mathfrak{a}_2) = (\mathfrak{c}_1, \mathfrak{c}_2)\,; \qquad (32.)$$

and these two steps $\mathfrak{c}_1\ \mathfrak{c}_2$ must each vary proportionally to the product $a_2\,\mathfrak{a}_2$, since otherwise it could be proved that the foregoing conditions, (27.) and (28.), would not be satisfied; we are, therefore, to suppose

$$\mathfrak{c}_1 = \gamma_1\,a_2\,\mathfrak{a}_2, \quad \mathfrak{c}_2 = \gamma_2\,a_2\,\mathfrak{a}_2, \qquad (33.)$$

that is,

$$(0, a_2)\ (0, \mathfrak{a}_2) = (\gamma_1\,a_2\,\mathfrak{a}_2,\ \gamma_2\,a_2\,\mathfrak{a}_2), \qquad (34.)$$

γ_1, γ_2, being some two constant numbers, independent of a_2 and $\mathfrak{a}_2$, but otherwise capable of being chosen at pleasure. Thus, the general formula for the product of a step-couple $(\mathfrak{a}_1, \mathfrak{a}_2)$ multiplied by a number-couple (a_1, a_2), is, by (31.) (34.) and by the theorem for sums,

$$(a_1, a_2)\ (\mathfrak{a}_1, \mathfrak{a}_2) = (a_1\,\mathfrak{a}_1,\ a_1\,\mathfrak{a}_2 + a_2\,\mathfrak{a}_1) + (\gamma_1\,a_2\,\mathfrak{a}_2,\ \gamma_2\,a_2\,\mathfrak{a}_2)$$

$$= (a_1\,\mathfrak{a}_1 + \gamma_1\,a_2\,\mathfrak{a}_2,\ a_1\,\mathfrak{a}_2 + a_2\,\mathfrak{a}_1 + \gamma_2\,a_2\,\mathfrak{a}_2): \qquad (35.)$$

and accordingly this formula satisfies the conditions (27.) and (28.), and includes the relations (22.) and (24.), whatever arbitrary numbers we choose for γ_1, and γ_2; provided that after once choosing these numbers, which we may call the *constants of multiplication*, we retain thenceforth unaltered, and treat them as independent of both the multiplier and the multiplicand. It is clear, however, that the simplicity and elegance of our future operations and results must mainly depend on our making a simple and suitable choice of these two constants of multiplication; and that in making this choice, we ought to take care to satisfy, if possible, the essential condition that there shall be always *one determined number-couple to express the ratio of any one determined step-couple to any other*, at least when the latter is not null : since this was the very object, to accomplish which we were led to introduce the conception of these number-couples. It is easy to show that no choice simpler than the following,

$$\gamma_1 = -1, \ \gamma_2 = 0, \qquad (36.)$$

would satisfy this essential condition : and for that reason we shall now select these two numbers, contra-positive one and zero, for the two constants of multiplication, and shall establish finally this formula for the multiplication of any step-couple $(\mathrm{a}_1, \mathrm{a}_2)$ by any number-couple (a_1, a_2),

$$(a_1, a_2)(\mathrm{a}_1, \mathrm{a}_2) = (a_1 \mathrm{a}_1 - a_2 \mathrm{a}_2, \ a_2 \mathrm{a}_1 + a_1 \mathrm{a}_2). \qquad (37.)$$

5. In fact, whatever constants of multiplication $\gamma_1 \ \gamma_2$ we may select, if we denote by $(\mathrm{b}_1, \mathrm{b}_2)$ the product of the step-couple $(\mathrm{a}_1, \mathrm{a}_2)$ by the number-couple (a_1, a_2), so that

$$(\mathrm{b}_1, \mathrm{b}_2) = (a_1, a_2) \times (\mathrm{a}_1, \mathrm{a}_2), \qquad (38.)$$

we have by (35.) the following expressions for the two coupled steps $\mathrm{b}_1, \mathrm{b}_2$, of the product,

$$\left.\begin{array}{l} \mathrm{b}_1 = a_1 \mathrm{a}_1 + \gamma_1 a_2 \mathrm{a}_2, \\ \mathrm{b}_2 = a_1 \mathrm{a}_2 + a_2 \mathrm{a}_1 + \gamma_2 a_2 \mathrm{a}_2, \end{array}\right\} \qquad (39.)$$

and therefore

$$\left.\begin{array}{l} \beta_1 = a_1 \alpha_1 + \gamma_1 a_2 \alpha_2, \\ \beta_2 = a_1 \alpha_2 + a_2 \alpha_1 + \gamma_2 a_2 \alpha_2, \end{array}\right\} \qquad (40.)$$

if $\alpha_1 \ \alpha_2 \ \beta_1 \ \beta_2$ denote respectively the ratios of the four steps $\mathrm{a}_1 \ \mathrm{a}_2 \ \mathrm{b}_1 \ \mathrm{b}_2$ to one effective step c, so that

$$\mathrm{a}_1 = \alpha_1 \mathrm{c}, \ \mathrm{a}_2 = \alpha_2 \mathrm{c}, \qquad (41.)$$

and

$$\mathrm{b}_1 = \beta_1 \mathrm{c}, \ \mathrm{b}_2 = \beta_2 \mathrm{c}; \qquad (42.)$$

from which it follows that

$$\left.\begin{array}{l} \alpha_1 \{a_1 (a_1 + \gamma_2 a_2) - \gamma_1 a_2^2\} = \beta_1 (a_1 + \gamma_2 a_2) - \beta_2 \gamma_1 a_2, \\ \alpha_2 \{a_1 (a^1 + \gamma_2 a_2) - \gamma_1 a_2^2\} = \beta_2 a^1 - \beta_1 a_2; \end{array}\right\} \qquad (43.)$$

in order therefore that the numbers $\alpha_1 \ \alpha_2$ should always be determined by the equation (38.), when a_1 and a_2 are not both null steps, it is necessary and sufficient that the factor

$$\alpha_1(\alpha_1+\gamma_2\alpha_2)-\gamma_1\alpha_2^2=(\alpha_1+\tfrac{1}{2}\gamma_2\alpha_2)^2-(\gamma_1+\tfrac{1}{4}\gamma_2^2)\alpha_2^2 \qquad (44.)$$

should never become null, when α_1 and α_2 are not both null numbers; and this condition will be satisfied if we so choose the constants of multiplication $\gamma_1\ \gamma_2$ as to make

$$\gamma_1+\tfrac{1}{4}\gamma_2^2<0, \qquad (45.)$$

but not otherwise. Whatever constants $\gamma_1\ \gamma_2$ we choose, we have, by the foregoing principles,

$$\frac{(c,0)}{(c,0)}=(1,0);\quad \frac{(0,c)}{(c,0)}=(0,1);\quad \frac{(0,c)}{(0,c)}=(1,0); \qquad (46.)$$

and finally

$$\frac{(c,0)}{(0,c)}=\left(-\frac{\gamma_2}{\gamma_1},\ \frac{1}{\gamma_1}\right), \qquad (47.)$$

because, when we make, in (43.),

$$\alpha_1=0,\ \alpha_2=1,\ \beta_1=1,\ \beta_2=0, \qquad (48.)$$

we find

$$a_1=\frac{-\gamma_2}{\gamma_1},\ a_2=\frac{1}{\gamma_1}; \qquad (49.)$$

so that although the ratio of the pure primary step-couple $(c,0)$ to the pure secondary step-couple $(0,c)$ can never be expressed as a *pure primary number-couple*, it may be expressed as a *pure secondary number-couple*, namely $(0,\frac{1}{\gamma_1})$, if we choose 0, as in (36.), for the value of the secondary constant γ_2, but not otherwise: this choice $\gamma_2=0$ is therefore required by simplicity. And since by the condition (45.), the primary constant γ_1 must be contrapositive, the simplest way of determining it is to make it contrapositive one, $\gamma_1=-1$, as announced in (36.). We have therefore justified that selection (36.) of the two constants of multiplication; and find, with that selection,

$$\frac{(c,0)}{(0,c)}=(0,-1), \qquad (50.)$$

and generally, for the ratio of any one step-couple to any other, the formula

$$\frac{(\mathrm{b}_1,\mathrm{b}_2)}{(\mathrm{a}_1,\mathrm{a}_2)}=\frac{(\beta_1 c,\beta_2 c)}{(\alpha_1 c,\alpha_2 c)}=\left(\frac{\beta_1\alpha_1+\beta_2\alpha_2}{\alpha_1^2+\alpha_2^2},\ \frac{\beta_2\alpha_1-\beta_1\alpha_2}{\alpha_1^2+\alpha_2^2}\right). \qquad (51.)$$

On the Addition, Subtraction, Multiplication, and Division, of Number-Couples, as combined with each other.

6. Proceeding to operations upon number-couples, considered in combination with each other, it is easy now to see the reasonableness of the following definitions, and even their necessity, if we would preserve in the simplest way, the analogy of the theory of couples to the theory of singles:

$$(b_1, b_2) + (a_1, a_2) = (b_1 + a_1, b_2 + a_2); \quad (52.)$$

$$(b_1, b_2) - (a_1, a_2) = (b_1 - a_1, b_2 - a_2); \quad (53.)$$

$$(b_1, b_2)(a_1, a_2) = (b_1, b_2) \times (a_1, a_2) = (b_1 a_1 - b_2 a_2, b_2 a_1 + b_1 a_2); \quad (54.)$$

$$\frac{(b_1, b_2)}{(a_1, a_2)} = \left(\frac{b_1 a_1 + b_2 a_2}{a_1^2 + a_2^2}, \frac{b_2 a_1 - b_1 a_2}{a_1^2 + a_2^2}\right). \quad (55.)$$

Were these definitions even altogether arbitrary, they would at least not contradict each other, nor the earlier principles of Algebra, and it would be possible to draw legitimate conclusions, by rigorous mathematical reasoning, from premises thus arbitrarily assumed: but the persons who have read with attention the foregoing remarks of this theory, and have compared them with the Preliminary Essay, will see that these definitions are really *not arbitrarily chosen*, and that though others might have been assumed, no others would be equally proper.

With these definitions, addition and subtraction of number-couples are mutually inverse operations, and so are multiplication and division; and we have the relations,

$$(b_1, b_2) + (a_1, a_2) = (a_1, a_2) + (b_1, b_2), \quad (56.)$$

$$(b_1, b_2) \times (a_1, a_2) = (a_1, a_2) \times (b_1, b_2), \quad (57.)$$

$$(b_1, b_2)\{(a'_1\, a'_2) + (a_1, a_2)\} = (b_1, b_2)\ (a'_1, a'_2) + (b_1, b_2)\ (a_1, a_2): \quad (58.)$$

we may, therefore, extend to number-couples all those results respecting numbers, which have been deduced from principles corresponding to these last relations. For example,

$$\{(b_1, b_2) + (a_1, a_2)\} \times \{(b_1, b_2) + (a_1, a_2)\} =$$

$$(b_1, b_2)\ (b_1, b_2) + 2\,(b_1, b_2)\ (a_1, a_2) + (a_1, a_2)\ (a_1, a_2), \quad (59.)$$

in which

$$2(b_1, b_2)(a_1, a_2) = (2, 0)(b_1, b_2)(a_1, a_2) = (b_1, b_2)(a_1, a_2) + (b_1, b_2)(a_1, a_2); \quad (60.)$$

for, in general, we may *mix the signs of numbers with those of number-couples*, if we consider every single number a as equivalent to a pure primary number-couple,

$$a = (a, 0). \quad (61.)$$

When the pure primary couple (1, 0) is thus considered as equivalent to the number 1, it may be called, for shortness, the *primary unit*; and the pure secondary couple (0, 1) may be called in like manner the *secondary unit*.

We may also agree to write, by analogy to notations already explained,

$$\left.\begin{array}{l}(0, 0) + (a_1, a_2) = +(a_1, a_2), \\ (0, 0) - (a_1, a_2) = -(a_1, a_2);\end{array}\right\} \quad (62.)$$

and then $+(a_1, a_2)$ will be another symbol for the number-couple (a_1, a_2) itself, and $-(a_1, a_2)$ will be a symbol for the *opposite number-couple* $(-a_1, -a_2)$. The *reciprocal* of a number-couple (a_1, a_2) is this other number-couple,

$$\frac{1}{(a_1, a_2)} = \frac{(1, 0)}{(a_1, a_2)} = \left(\frac{a_1}{a_1^2 + a_2^2}, \frac{-a_2}{a_1^2 + a_2^2}\right) = \frac{(a_1, -a_2)}{a_1^2 + a_2^2}. \quad (63.)$$

It need scarcely be mentioned that the insertion of the sign of coincidence $=$ between any two number-couples implies that those two couples coincide, number with number, primary with primary, and secondary with secondary; so that *an equation between number-couples is equivalent to a couple of equations between numbers.*

On the Powering of a Number-couple by Single Whole Number.

7. Any number-couple (a_1, a_2) may be used as a *base* to generate a series of *powers*, with integer *exponents*, or *logarithms*, namely, the series

$$\ldots (a_1, a_2)^{-2}, (a_1, a_2)^{-1}, (a_1, a_2)^0, (a_1, a_2)^1, (a_1, a_2)^2, \ldots \quad (64.)$$

in which the *first positive power* $(a_1, a_2)^1$ is the base itself, and all the others are formed from it by repeated multiplication or division by that base, according as they follow or precede it in the series; thus,

$$(a_1, a_2)^0 = (1, 0), \quad (65.)$$

and

$$\left.\begin{array}{ll}(a_1, a_2)^1 = (a_1, a_2), & (a_1, a_2)^{-1} = \dfrac{(1, 0)}{(a_1, a_2)}, \\ (a_1, a_2)^2 = (a_1, a_2)\,(a_1, a_2), & (a_1, a_2)^{-2} = \dfrac{(1, 0)}{(a_1, a_2)\,(a_1, a_2)}, \\ \&c. & \&c.\end{array}\right\} \qquad (66.)$$

To *power* the couple (a_1, a_2) by any *positive* whole number m, is, therefore, to *multiply*, m times successively, the *primary unit*, or the couple $(1, 0)$, by the proposed couple (a_1, a_2); and to power (a_1, a_2) by any *contra-positive* whole number $-m$, is to *divide* $(1, 0)$ by the same couple (a_1, a_2), m times successively: but to power by 0 produces always $(1, 0.)$. Hence, generally, for any whole numbers μ, ν,

$$\left.\begin{array}{c}(a_1, a_2)^{\mu}\,(a_1, a_2)^{\nu} = (a_1, a_2)^{\mu+\nu}, \\ ((a_1, a_2)^{\mu})^{\nu} = (a_1, a_2)^{\mu\nu}.\end{array}\right\} \qquad (67.)$$

8. In the theory of single numbers,

$$\frac{(a+b)^m}{1\times2\times3\ldots\times m} = \frac{a^m}{1\times2\times3\ldots\times m} + \frac{a^{m-1}}{1\times2\times3\times\ldots(m-1)}\,\frac{b^1}{1} + \frac{a^{m-2}}{1\times2\times3\times\ldots(m-2)}\,\frac{b^2}{1\times2} + \ldots$$
$$+ \frac{a^1}{1}\,\frac{b^{m-1}}{1\times2\times3\times\ldots(m-1)} + \frac{b^m}{1\times2\times3\times\ldots m}; \qquad (68.)$$

and similarly in the theory of number-couples,

$$\frac{\{(a_1, a_2) + (b_1, b_2)\}^m}{1\times2\times3\times\ldots m} = \frac{(a_1, a_2)^m}{1\times2\times3\times\ldots m} + \frac{(a_1, a_2)^{m-1}}{1\times2\times3\times\ldots(m-1)}\,\frac{(b_1, b_2)^1}{1}$$
$$+ \frac{(a_1, a_2)^{m-2}}{1\times2\times3\times\ldots(m-2)}\,\frac{(b_1, b_2)^2}{1\times2} + \ldots$$
$$+ \frac{(a_1, a_2)^1}{1}\,\frac{(b_1, b_2)^{m-1}}{1\times2\times3\times\ldots(m-1)} + \frac{(b_1, b_2)^m}{1\times2\times3\times\ldots m}; \qquad (69.)$$

m being in both these formulæ a positive whole number, but $a\ b\ a_1\ a_2\ b_1\ b_2$ being any numbers whatever. The latter formula, which includes the former, may easily be proved by considering the product of m unequal factor sums,

$$(a_1, a_2) + (b_1^{(1)}, b_2^{(1)}),\ (a_1, a_2) + (b_1^{(2)}, b_2^{(2)}), \ldots\ (a_1, a_2) + (b_1^{(m)}, b_2^{(m)}); \qquad (70.)$$

for, in this product, when developed by the rules of multiplication, the power $(a_1, a_2)^{m-n}$ is multiplied by the sum of all the products of n factor couples such as $(b_1^{(1)}, b_2^{(1)})$ $(b_1^{(2)}, b_2^{(2)})\ldots(b_1^{(n)}, b_2^{(n)})$; and the number of such products is the number of combinations of m things, taken n by n, that is,

$$\frac{1\times 2\times 3\times\ldots\times m}{1\times 2\times 3\times\ldots(m-n)\times 1\times 2\times 3\times\ldots n}, \qquad (71.)$$

while these products themselves become each $=(b_1, b_2)^n$, when we return to the case of equal factors.

The formula (69.) enables us to determine separately the primary and secondary numbers of the power or couple $(a_1, a_2)^m$, by treating the base (a_1, a_2) as the sum of a pure primary couple $(a_1, 0)$ and a pure secondary $(0, a_2)$, and by observing that the powering of these latter number-couples may be performed by multiplying the powers of the numbers a_1 a_2 by the powers of the primary and secondary units, $(1, 0)$ and $(0, 1)$; for, whatever whole number i may be,

$$\left.\begin{aligned}(a_1, 0)^i &= a_1^i\,(1, 0)^i,\\ (0, a_2)^i &= a_2^i\,(0, 1)^i.\end{aligned}\right\} \qquad (72.)$$

We have also the following expressions for the powers of these two units,

$$\left.\begin{aligned}(1, 0)^i &= (1, 0);\\ (0, 1)^{4k-3} &= (0, 1),\\ (0, 1)^{4k-2} &= (-1, 0),\\ (0, 1)^{4k-1} &= (0, -1),\\ (0, 1)^{4k} &= (1, 0);\end{aligned}\right\} \qquad (73.)$$

that is, the powers of the primary unit are all themselves equal to that primary unit; but the first, second, third, and fourth powers of the secondary unit are respectively

$$(0, 1)\ (-1, 0),\ (0, -1),\ (1, 0);$$

and the higher powers are formed by merely repeating this period. In like manner we find that the equation

$$(a_1, a_2)^m = (b_1, b_2), \qquad (74.)$$

is equivalent to the two following,

$$\left.\begin{aligned}b_1 &= a_1^{m} - \frac{m\,(m-1)}{1\times 2}\,a_1^{m-2}\,a_2^2 + \frac{m\,(m-1)\,(m-2)\,(m-3)}{1\times 2\times 3\times 4}\,a_1^{m-4}a_2^4 - \text{\&c.}\\ b_2 &= m\,a_1^{m-1}\,a_2 - \frac{m\,(m-1)\,(m-2)}{1\times 2\times 3}\,a_1^{m-3}a_2^3 + \text{\&c.}\end{aligned}\right\} \qquad (75.)$$

For example, the square and cube of a couple, that is, the second and third positive powers of it, may be developed thus,

$$(a_1, a_2)^2 = \{(a_1, 0) + (0, a_2)\}^2 = (a_1^2 - a_2^2,\ 2\,a_1\,a_2), \qquad (76.)$$

and

$$(a_1, a_2)^3 = \{(a_1, 0) + (0, a_2)\}^3 = (a_1^3 - 3a_1 a_2^2,\ 3a_1^2 a_2 - a_2^3). \qquad (77.)$$

9. In general, if

$$(a_1, a_2)\ (a'_1, a'_2) = (a''_1, a''_2), \qquad (78.)$$

then, by the theorem or rule of multiplication (54.)

$$a''_1 = a_1 a'_1 - a_2 a'_2,\quad a''_2 = a_2 a'_1 + a_1 a'_2, \qquad (79.)$$

and therefore

$$a''^2_1 + a''^2_2 = (a_1^2 + a_2^2)\ (a'^2_1 + a'^2_2); \qquad (80.)$$

and in like manner it may be proved that

$$\left.\begin{array}{l} \text{if } (a_1, a_2)\ (a'_1, a'_2)\ (a''_1, a''_2) = (a'''_1, a'''_2), \\ \text{then } (a'''^2_1 + a'''^2_2) = (a_1^2 + a_2^2)\ (a'^2_1 + a'^2_2)\ (a''^2_1 + a''^2_2), \end{array}\right\} \qquad (81.)$$

and so on, for any number m of factors. Hence, in particular, when all these m factors are equal, so that the product becomes a power, and the equation (74.) is satisfied, the two numbers b_1 b_2 of the *power-couple* must be connected with the two numbers a_1 a_2 of the *base-couple* by the relation

$$b_1^2 + b_2^2 = (a_1^2 + a_2^2)^m. \qquad (82.)$$

For example, in the cases of the square and cube, this relation holds good under the forms

$$(a_1^2 - a_2^2)^2 + (2a_1 a_2)^2 = (a_1^2 + a_2^2)^2, \qquad (83.)$$

and

$$(a_1^3 - 3a_1 a_2^2)^2 + (3a_1^2 a_2 - a_2^3)^2 = (a_1^2 + a_2^2)^3. \qquad (84.)$$

The relation (82.) is true even for powers with contra-positive exponents $-m$, that is,

$$b_1^2 + b_2^2 = (a_1^2 + a_2^2)^{-m} \text{ if } (b_1, b_2) = (a_1, a_2)^{-m}; \qquad (85.)$$

for in general

$$\left.\begin{array}{l} \text{if } (b_1, b_2) = \dfrac{(a_1, a_2)\ (a'_1, a'_2)\ (a''_1, a''_2) \dots}{(c_1, c_2)\ (c'_1, c'_2)\ (c''_1, c''_2) \dots} \\ \text{then } (b_1^2 + b_2^2) = \dfrac{(a_1^2 + a_2^2)\ (a'^2_1 + a'^2_2)\ (a''^2_1 + a''^2_2) \dots}{(c_1^2 + c_2^2)\ (c'^2_1 + c'^2_2)\ (c''^2_1 + c''^2_2) \dots} \end{array}\right\} \qquad (86.)$$

On a particular Class of Exponential and Logarithmic Function-Couples, connected with a particular Series of Integer Powers of Number-Couples.

10. The theorem (69.) shows, that if we employ the symbols $F_m(a_1, a_2)$ and $F_m(b_1, b_2)$ to denote concisely two number-couples, which depend in the following way on the couples (a_1, a_2) and (b_1, b_2),

$$F_m(a_1, a_2) = (1, 0) + \frac{(a_1, a_2)^1}{1} + \frac{(a_1, a_2)^2}{1\times 2} + \dots + \frac{(a_1, a_2)^m}{1\times 2\times 3\times \dots m}, \qquad (87.)$$

$$F_m(b_1, b_2) = (1, 0) + \frac{(b_1, b_2)^1}{1} + \frac{(b_1, b_2)^2}{1\times 2} + \dots + \frac{(b_1, b_2)^m}{1\times 2\times 3\times \dots m}, \qquad (88.)$$

and if we denote in like manner by the symbol

$$F_m((a_1, a_2) + (b_1, b_2)) = F_m(a_1 + b_1, a_2 + b_2) \qquad (89.)$$

the couple which depends in the same way on the sum $(a_1, a_2) + (b_1, b_2)$, or on the couple $(a_1 + b_1, a_2 + b_2)$, and develope by the rule (69.) the powers of this latter sum, we shall have the relation

$$\begin{aligned} &\{F_m(a_1, a_2) \times F_m(b_1, b_2)\} - F_m((a_1, a_2) + (b_1, b_2)) = \\ &\frac{(a_1, a_2)^m}{1\times 2\times 3\times \dots m}\left\{\frac{(b_1, b_2)^1}{1} + \frac{(b_1, b_2)^2}{1\times 2} + \dots + \frac{(b_1, b_2)^m}{1\times 2\times 3\times \dots m}\right\} \\ &+ \frac{(a_1, a_2)^{m-1}}{1\times 2\times 3\times \dots (m-1)}\left\{\frac{(b_1, b_2)^2}{1\times 2} + \dots + \frac{(b_1, b_2)^m}{1\times 2\times 3\times \dots m}\right\} \\ &+ \dots\dots \\ &+ \frac{(a_1, a_2)^1}{1}\,\frac{(b_1, b_2)^m}{1\times 2\times 3\times \dots m}. \end{aligned} \qquad (90.)$$

This expression may be farther developed, by the rule for the multiplication of a sum, into the sum of several terms or couples, (c_1, c_2), of which the number is

$$1 + 2 + 3 + \dots + m = \frac{m(m+1)}{2}, \qquad (91.)$$

and which are of the form

$$(c_1, c_2) = \frac{(a_1, a_2)^i}{1\times 2\times 3\times \dots i} \times \frac{(b_1, b_2)^k}{1\times 2\times 3\times \dots k}, \qquad (92.)$$

i and k being positive integers, such that

$$i \not> m, \quad k \not> m, \quad i+k>m; \qquad (93.)$$

and if we put for abridgment

$$\sqrt{a_1^2+a_2^2}=a, \quad \sqrt{b_1^2+b_2^2}=\beta, \qquad (94.)$$

and

$$\gamma = \frac{a^i \beta^k}{1\times2\times3\times\ldots i\times1\times2\times3\times\ldots k}, \qquad (95.)$$

we shall have, by principles lately explained,

$$\sqrt{c_1^2+c_2^2}=\gamma, \qquad (96.)$$

and therefore

$$c_1 \not> +\gamma, \quad c_1 \not< -\gamma, \quad c_2 \not> +\gamma, \quad c_2 \not< -\gamma: \qquad (97.)$$

if then the entire sum (90.) of all these couples (c_1, c_2) be put under the form

$$\Sigma(c_1, c_2) = (\Sigma c_1, \Sigma c_2), \qquad (98.)$$

the letter Σ being used as a mark of summation, we shall have the corresponding limitations

$$\left.\begin{array}{l} \Sigma c_1 \not> \Sigma\gamma, \quad \Sigma c_1 \not< -\Sigma\gamma, \\ \Sigma c_2 \not> \Sigma\gamma, \quad \Sigma c_2 \not< -\Sigma\gamma, \end{array}\right\} \qquad (99.)$$

$\Sigma\gamma$ being the positive sum of the $\frac{m(m+1)}{2}$ such terms as that marked (95.). This latter sum depends on the positive whole number m, and on the positive numbers a, β; but whatever these two latter numbers may be, it is easy to show that by taking the former number sufficiently great, we can make the positive sum $\Sigma\gamma$ become smaller, that is nearer to 0, than any positive number δ previously assigned, however small that number δ may be. For if we use the symbols $F_m(a)$, $F_m(\beta)$, $F_m(a+\beta)$, to denote positive numbers connected with the positive numbers a, β, $a+\beta$, by relations analogous to those marked (87.) and (88.), so that

$$F_m(a) = 1 + \frac{a}{1} + \frac{a^2}{1\times2} + \ldots + \frac{a^m}{1\times2\times3\times\ldots m}, \qquad (100.)$$

it is easy to prove, by (68.), that the product $F_m(a) \times F_m(\beta)$ exceeds the number

$F_m(\alpha+\beta)$ by $\Sigma\gamma$, but falls short of the number $F_{2m}(\alpha+\beta)$, that is of the following number

$$F_{2m}(\alpha+\beta) = 1 + \frac{(\alpha+\beta)^1}{1} + \frac{(\alpha+\beta)^2}{1\times 2} + \ldots + \frac{(\alpha+\beta)^{2m}}{1\times 2\times 3\times\ldots\times 2m}; \quad (101.)$$

so that

$$\Sigma\gamma = (F_m(\alpha)\times F_m(\beta)) - F_m(\alpha+\beta), \quad (102.)$$

and

$$\Sigma\gamma < F_{2m}(\alpha+\beta) - F_m(\alpha+\beta): \quad (103.)$$

if then we choose a positive integer n, so as to satisfy the condition

$$n+1 > 2(\alpha+\beta), \text{ that is } \frac{\alpha+\beta}{n+1} < \tfrac{1}{2}, \quad (104.)$$

and take $m > n$, we shall have

$$\frac{(\alpha+\beta)^m}{1\times 2\times 3\times\ldots m} < \frac{1}{2^{m-n}}\,\frac{(\alpha+\beta)^n}{1\times 2\times 3\times\ldots n}, \text{ and therefore } < \delta, \quad (105.)$$

however small the positive number δ may be, and however large $\alpha+\beta$ may be, if we take m large enough; but also

$$F_{2m}(\alpha+\beta) - F_m(\alpha+\beta) = \frac{(\alpha+\beta)^m\eta}{1\times 2\times 3\times\ldots m} \text{ and therefore } < \delta\times\eta, \quad (106.)$$

in which

$$\eta = \frac{\alpha+\beta}{m+1} + \frac{(\alpha+\beta)^2}{(m+1)(m+2)} + \ldots + \frac{(\alpha+\beta)^m}{(m+1)(m+2)\times\ldots(2m)}, \quad (107.)$$

and, therefore,

$$\eta < 1, \quad (108.)$$

because

$$\frac{\alpha+\beta}{m+1} < \tfrac{1}{2}, \quad \frac{(\alpha+\beta)^2}{(m+1)(m+2)} < \frac{1}{2^2}, \ldots \frac{(\alpha+\beta)^m}{(m+1)(m+2)\times\ldots(2m)} < \frac{1}{2^m}; \quad (109.)$$

therefore, combining the inequalities (103.) (106.) (108.), we find finally

$$\Sigma\gamma < \delta. \quad (110.)$$

And hence, by (99.), the two sums Σc_1, Σc_2, may both be made to approach as near as we desire to 0, by taking m sufficiently large; so that, in the notation of limits already employed,

$$\underline{\text{L}}\,\Sigma\gamma = 0, \quad \underline{\text{L}}\,\Sigma c_1 = 0, \quad \underline{\text{L}}\,\Sigma c_2 = 0, \quad (111.)$$

and, therefore,

$$\mathrm{L}\left\{\mathrm{F}_m(\alpha)\cdot\mathrm{F}_m(\beta)-\mathrm{F}_m(\alpha+\beta)\right\}=0, \qquad (112.)$$

$$\mathrm{L}\left\{\mathrm{F}_m(a_1, a_2)\ \mathrm{F}_m(b_1, b_2)-\mathrm{F}_m\big((a_1, a_2)+(b_1, b_2)\big)\right\}=(0, 0). \qquad (113.)$$

In the foregoing investigation, α and β denoted positive numbers; but the theorem (113.) shows that the formula (112.) holds good, whatever numbers may be denoted by α and β, if we still interpret the symbol $\mathrm{F}_m(\alpha)$ by the rule (100.).

11. If α still retain the signification (94.), it results, from the foregoing reasonings, that the primary and secondary numbers of the couple

$$\mathrm{F}_{m+m'}(a_1, a_2)-\mathrm{F}_m(a_1, a_2) \qquad (114.)$$

are each

$$\not> \mathrm{F}_{m+m'}(\alpha)-\mathrm{F}_m(\alpha), \text{ and } \not< \mathrm{F}_m(\alpha)-\mathrm{F}_{m+m'}(\alpha); \qquad (115.)$$

and, therefore, may each be made nearer to 0 (on the positive or on the contra-positive side) than any proposed positive number δ by choosing m large enough, however large m' and α may be, and however small δ may be: because in the expression

$$\mathrm{F}_{m+m'}(\alpha)-\mathrm{F}_m(\alpha)=\frac{\alpha^m}{1\times2\times3\times\ldots m}\left\{\frac{\alpha}{m+1}+\frac{\alpha^2}{(m+1)(m+2)}+\ldots+\frac{\alpha^{m'}}{(m+1)\ldots(m+m')}\right\} \quad (116.)$$

the positive factor $\frac{\alpha^m}{1\times2\times3\times\ldots m}$ may be made $<\delta$, that is, as near as we please to 0, and also the other factor, as being $<\frac{1}{n}+\frac{1}{n^2}+\ldots+\frac{1}{n^{m'}}$, and therefore $<\frac{1}{n-1}$, if $m+1>n\,\alpha$. Pursuing this train of reasoning, we find that as m becomes greater and greater without end, the couple $\mathrm{F}_m(a_1, a_2)$ tends to a determinate *limit-couple*, which depends on the couple (a_1, a_2), and may be denoted by the symbol $\mathrm{F}_\infty(a_1, a_2)$, or simply $\mathrm{F}(a_1, a_2)$,

$$\mathrm{F}(a_1, a_2)=\mathrm{F}_\infty(a_1, a_2)=\mathrm{L}\ \mathrm{F}_m(a_1, a_2); \qquad (117.)$$

and similarly, that for any determinate number α, whether positive or not, the number $\mathrm{F}_m(\alpha)$ tends to a determinate *limit-number*, which depends on the number α, and may be denoted thus,

$$\mathrm{F}(\alpha)=\mathrm{F}_\infty(\alpha)=\mathrm{L}\ \mathrm{F}_m(\alpha). \qquad (118.)$$

It is easy also to prove, by (112.), that this *function*, or *dependent number*, $\mathrm{F}(\alpha)$, must always satisfy the conditions

$$\mathrm{F}(\alpha)\times\mathrm{F}(\beta)=\mathrm{F}(\alpha+\beta), \qquad (119.)$$

and that it increases constantly and continuously from positive states indefinitely near to 0 to positive states indefinitely far from 0, while a increases or advances constantly, and continuously, and indefinitely in the progression from contra-positive to positive; so that, for every positive number β, there is some determined number a which satisfies the condition

$$\beta = \text{F}(a), \qquad (120.)$$

and which may be thus denoted,

$$a = \text{F}^{-1}(\beta). \qquad (121.)$$

It may also be easily proved that we have always the relations,

$$\text{F}(a) = \underset{\circ}{e}^{a}, \quad \text{F}^{-1}(\beta) = \log_{e}.\ \beta, \qquad (122.)$$

if we put, for abridgement,

$$\text{F}(1) = e, \qquad (123.)$$

and employ the notation of powers and logarithms explained in the Preliminary Essay. A power $\underset{\circ}{b}^{a}$, when considered as depending on its exponent, is called an *exponential function* thereof; its most general and essential properties are those expressed by the formulæ,

$$\underset{\circ}{b}^{a} \times \underset{\circ}{b}^{\beta} = \underset{\circ}{b}^{a+\beta}, \quad \underset{\circ}{b}^{1} = b, \qquad (124.)$$

of which the first is independent of the base b, while the second specifies that base; and since, by (113.), the function-couple $\text{F}(a_1, a_2)$ satisfies the analogous condition,

$$\text{F}(a_1, a_2) \times \text{F}(b_1, b_2) = \text{F}\big((a_1, a_2) + (b_1, b_2)\big) = \text{F}(a_1 + b_1, a_2 + b_2), \qquad (125.)$$

(whatever numbers $a_1\ a_2\ b_1\ b_2$ may be,) we may say by analogy that this function-couple $\text{F}(a_1, a_2)$ is an *exponential function-couple*, and that its *base-couple* is

$$\text{F}(1, 0) = (e, 0): \qquad (126.)$$

and because the exponent a of a power $\underset{\circ}{b}^{a}$, when considered as depending on that power, is called a *logarithmic function* thereof; we may say by analogy that the couple (a_1, a_2) is a *logarithmic function*, or *function-couple*, of the couple $\text{F}(a_1, a_2)$, and may denote it thus,

$$(a_1, a_2) = \text{F}^{-1}(b_1, b_2), \quad \text{if} \quad (b_1, b_2) = \text{F}(a_1, a_2). \qquad (127.)$$

In general, if we can discover any law of dependence of one couple $\Phi\,(a_1, a_2)$, upon another (a_1, a_2), such that for all values of the numbers $a_1\ a_2\ b_1\ b_2$ the condition

$$\Phi\,(a_1, a_2)\ \Phi\,(b_1, b_2) = \Phi\,(a_1 + a_2,\ b_1 + b_2) \qquad (128.)$$

is satisfied, then, whether this function-couple $\Phi\,(a_1, a_2)$ be or be not coincident with the particular function-couple $\text{F}\,(a_1, a_2)$, we may call it (by the same analogy of definition) an *exponential function-couple*, calling the particular couple $\Phi\,(1, 0)$ its *base*, or *base-couple;* and may call the couple (a_1, a_2), when considered as depending inversely on $\Phi\,(a_1, a_2)$, a *logarithmic function*, or *function-couple*, which we may thus denote,

$$(a_1, a_2) = \Phi^{-1}(b_1, b_2), \text{ if } (b_1, b_2) = \Phi\,(a_1, a_2). \qquad (129.)$$

12. We have shown that the particular exponential function-couple $(b_1, b_2) = \text{F}\,(a_1, a_2)$ is always possible and determinate, whatever determinate couple (a_1, a_2) may be; let us now consider whether, inversely, the particular logarithmic function-couple $(a_1, a_2) = \text{F}^{-1}\,(b_1, b_2)$ is always possible and determinate, for every determined couple (b_1, b_2). By the exponential properties of the function F, we have

$$(b_1, b_2) = \text{F}\,(a_1, a_2) = \text{F}\,(a_1, 0)\ \text{F}\,(0, a_2) = \text{F}\,(a_1)\ \text{F}\,(0, a_2)$$
$$= (\overset{\circ}{e}{}^{a_1} \cos a_2,\ \overset{\circ}{e}{}^{a_1} \sin a_2), \qquad (130.)$$

if we define the functions cos a and sin a, or more fully the *cosine* and *sine* of any number a, to be the primary and secondary numbers of the couple $\text{F}\,(0, a)$, or the numbers which satisfy the *couple-equation*,

$$\text{F}\,(0, a) = (\cos a, \sin a). \qquad (131.)$$

From this definition, or from these two others which it includes, namely from the following expressions of the functions *cosine* and *sine* as limits of the sums of series, which are already familiar to mathematicians,

$$\left.\begin{aligned} \cos a &= 1 - \frac{a^2}{1\times 2} + \frac{a^4}{1\times 2\times 3\times 4} - \&c. \\ \sin a &= a - \frac{a^3}{1\times 2\times 3} + \frac{a^5}{1\times 2\times 3\times 4\times 5} - \&c. \end{aligned}\right\} \qquad (132.)$$

it is possible to deduce all the other known properties of these two functions; and especially that they are *periodical functions*, in such a manner that while the variable number a increases constantly and continuously from 0 to a certain constant positive number $\frac{\pi}{2}$, (π being a certain number between 3 and 4,) the function $\sin a$ increases with it (constantly and continuously) from 0 to 1, but $\cos a$ decreases (constantly and continuously) from 1 to 0; while a continues to increase from $\frac{\pi}{2}$ to π, $\sin a$ decreases from 1 to 0, and $\cos a$ from 0 to -1; while a increases from π to $\frac{3\pi}{2}$, $\sin a$ decreases from 0 to -1, but $\cos a$ increases from -1 to 0; while a still increases from $\frac{3\pi}{2}$ to 2π, $\sin a$ increases from -1 to 0, and $\cos a$ from 0 to 1, the sum of the squares of the cosine and sine remaining always $= 1$; and that then the same changes recur in the same order, having also occurred before for contra-positive values of a, according to this *law of periodicity*, that

$$\cos(a \pm 2i\pi) = \cos a, \quad \sin(a \pm 2i\pi) = \sin a, \qquad (133.)$$

i denoting here (as elsewhere in the present paper) any positive whole number. But because the proof of these well known properties may be deduced from the equations (132.), without any special reference to the theory of couples, it is not necessary, and it might not be proper, to dwell upon it here.

It is, however, important to observe here, that by these properties we can always find (or conceive found) an indefinite variety of numbers a, differing from each other by multiples of the constant number 2π, and yet each having its cosine equal to any one proposed number β_1, and its sine equal to any other proposed number β_2, provided that the sum of the squares of these two proposed numbers β_1, β_2, is $= 1$; and reciprocally, that if two different numbers a both satisfy the conditions

$$\cos a = \beta_1, \quad \sin a = \beta_2, \qquad (134.)$$

β_1 and β_2 being two given numbers, such that $\beta_1^2 + \beta_2^2 = 1$, then the difference of these two numbers a is necessarily a multiple of 2π. Among all these numbers a, there will always be one which will satisfy these other conditions

$$a > -\pi, \quad a \ngtr \pi, \qquad (135.)$$

and this particular number a may be called the *principal solution* of the equations (134.), because it is always nearer to 0 than any other number a which satisfies the same equations, except in the particular case when $\beta_1 = -1$, $\beta_2 = 0$; and because, in this particular case, though the two numbers π and $-\pi$ are equally near to 0, and both satisfy the equations (134.), yet still the principal solution π, assigned by the conditions (135.), is simpler than the other solution $-\pi$, which is rejected by those last conditions. It is therefore always possible to find not only one, but infinitely many number-couples (a_1, a_2), differing from each other by multiples of the constant couple (0, 2π), but satisfying each the equation (130.), and therefore each entitled to be represented by, or included in the meaning of, the general symbol $F^{-1}(b_1, b_2)$, whatever proposed effective couple (b_1, b_2) may be. For we have only to satisfy, by (130.), the two separate equations

$$\underset{\circ}{e}^{a_1} \cos a_2 = b_1, \ \underset{\circ}{e}^{a_1} \sin a_2 = b_2; \qquad (136.)$$

which are equivalent to the three following,

$$\underset{\circ}{e}^{a_1} = \sqrt{b_1^2 + b_2^2}, \qquad (137.)$$

and

$$\cos a_2 = \frac{b_1}{\sqrt{b_1^2 + b_2^2}}, \ \sin a_2 = \frac{b_2}{\sqrt{b_1^2 + b_2^2}}; \qquad (138.)$$

and if a be the *principal solution* of these two last equations, we shall have as their most general solution

$$a_2 = a + 2\omega\pi, \qquad (139.)$$

while the formula (137.) gives

$$a_1 = \log_e . \sqrt{b_1^2 + b_2^2}: \qquad (140.)$$

the couple (a_1, a_2) admits therefore of all the following values, consistently with the conditions (130.) or (136.),

$$(a_1, a_2) = F^{-1}(b_1, b_2) = (\log_e . \sqrt{b_1^2 + b_2^2}, \ a + 2\omega\pi), \qquad (141.)$$

in which ω is any whole number, and a is a number $> -\pi$, but not $> \pi$, which has its cosine and sine respectively equal to the proposed numbers b_1, b_2, divided each by the square-root of the sum of their squares. To specify any one value of (a_1, a_2), or $F^{-1}(b_1, b_2)$, corresponding to any one particular whole number ω, we may use the symbol $\underset{\omega}{F}^{-1}(b_1, b_2)$; and then the symbol $\underset{\circ}{F}^{-1}(b_1, b_2)$ will denote what may be called the *principal value* of the inverse or logarithmic function-couple $F^{-1}(b_1, b_2)$, because it corresponds to the principal value of the number a_2, as determined by the conditions (138.).

On the Powering of any Number-Couple by any Single Number or Number-Couple.

13. Resuming now the problem of powering a number-couple by a number, we may employ this property of the exponential function F,

$$(\text{F}(a_1, a_2))^\mu = \text{F}(\mu a_1, \mu a_2), \qquad (142.)$$

μ being any whole number whether positive or contrapositive or null; which easily follows from (125.), and gives this expression for the μ'th power, or *power-couple*, of any effective number-couple,

$$(b_1, b_2)^\mu = \text{F}(\mu\, \text{F}^{-1}(b_1, b_2)). \qquad (143.)$$

Reciprocally if (a_1, a_2) be an mth root, or *root-couple*, of a proposed couple (b_1, b_2), so that the equation (74.) is satisfied, then

$$(a_1, a_2) = (b_1, b_2)^{\frac{1}{m}} = \text{F}\left(\frac{1}{m}\, \text{F}^{-1}(b_1, b_2)\right). \qquad (144.)$$

This last expression admits of many values, when the positive whole number m is >1, on account of the indeterminateness of the inverse or logarithmic function F^{-1}; and to specify any one of these values of the root-couple, corresponding to any one value $\underset{\omega}{\text{F}^{-1}}$ of that inverse function, which value of the root we may call *the ωth value* of that root, we may employ the notation

$$\underset{\omega}{(b_1, b_2)^{\frac{1}{m}}} = \text{F}\left(\frac{1}{m}\, \underset{\omega}{\text{F}^{-1}}(b_1, b_2)\right); \qquad (145.)$$

we may also call the particular value

$$\underset{0}{(b_1, b_2)^{\frac{1}{m}}} = \text{F}\left(\frac{1}{m}\, \underset{0}{\text{F}^{-1}}(b_1, b_2)\right), \qquad (146.)$$

the *principal value* of the root-couple, or the *principal m'th root* of the couple (b_1, b_2). In this notation,

$$\underset{\omega}{(1, 0)^{\frac{1}{m}}} = \text{F}\left(0, \frac{2\omega\pi}{m}\right), \qquad (147.)$$

$$\underset{\omega}{(b_1, b_2)^{\frac{1}{m}}} = \underset{0}{(b_1, b_2)^{\frac{1}{m}}}\ \underset{\omega}{(1, 0)^{\frac{1}{m}}}; \qquad (148.)$$

so that generally, *the ω'th value of the m th root of any number-couple is equal to the principal value of that root multiplied by the ωth value of the m th root of the* *primary unit* (1, 0). The mth root of any couple has therefore *m distinct values*, and no more, because the mth root of the primary unit (1, 0) has m distinct values, and no more, since it may be thus expressed, by (147.) and (131.),

$$(1, 0)^{\frac{1}{m}}_{\omega} = \left(\cos. \frac{2\,\omega\,\pi}{m}, \ \sin. \frac{2\,\omega\,\pi}{m} \right), \qquad (149.)$$

so that, by the law of periodicity (133.), for any different whole number ω',

$$(1, 0)^{\frac{1}{m}}_{\omega'} = (1, 0)^{\frac{1}{m}}_{\omega}, \qquad (150.)$$

and therefore generally,

$$(b_1, b_2)^{\frac{1}{m}}_{\omega'} = (b_1, b_2)^{\frac{1}{m}}_{\omega}, \qquad (151.)$$

if

$$\omega' = \omega \pm i\,m, \qquad (152.)$$

but not otherwise. For example, the cube-root of the primary unit (1, 0) has three distinct values, and no more, namely

$$(1, 0)^{\frac{1}{3}}_{0} = (1, 0)\,;\ (1, 0)^{\frac{1}{3}}_{1} = \left(-\frac{1}{2}, \frac{\sqrt{3}}{2}\right);\ (1, 0)^{\frac{1}{3}}_{2} = \left(-\frac{1}{2}, -\frac{\sqrt{3}}{2}\right); \qquad (153.)$$

so that each of these three couples, but no other, has its cube $=$ (1, 0). Again the couple (−1, 0) has two distinct square-roots, and no more, namely

$$(-1, 0)^{\frac{1}{2}}_{0} = (0, 1)\,;\ (-1, 0)^{\frac{1}{2}}_{1} = (0, -1). \qquad (154.)$$

In general we may agree to denote the *principal square-root* of a couple (b_1, b_2) by the symbol

$$\sqrt{(b_1, b_2)} = (b_1, b_2)^{\frac{1}{2}}_{0}; \qquad (155.)$$

and then we shall have the particular equation

$$\sqrt{(-1, 0)} = (0, 1)\,; \qquad (156.)$$

which may, by the principle (61.), be concisely denoted as follows,

$$\sqrt{-1} = (0, 1). \qquad (157.)$$

In the THEORY OF SINGLE NUMBERS, the symbol $\sqrt{-1}$ is *absurd*, and denotes an IMPOSSIBLE EXTRACTION, or a merely IMAGINARY NUMBER; but in the THEORY OF COUPLES, the same symbol $\sqrt{-1}$ is *significant*, and denotes a POSSIBLE EXTRACTION, or a REAL COUPLE, namely (as we have just now seen) the *principal square-root of the couple* $(-1, 0)$. In the latter theory, therefore, though not in the former, this sign $\sqrt{-1}$ may properly be employed; and we may write, if we choose, for any couple (a_1, a_2) whatever,

$$(a_1, a_2) = a_1 + a_2 \sqrt{-1}, \qquad (158.)$$

interpreting the symbols a_1 and a_2, in the expression $a_1 + a_2 \sqrt{-1}$, as denoting the pure primary couples $(a_1, 0)$ $(a_2, 0)$, according to the law of mixture (61.) of numbers with number-couples, and interpreting the symbol $\sqrt{-1}$, in the same expression, as denoting the secondary unit or pure secondary couple $(0, 1)$, according to the formula (157.). However, the notation (a_1, a_2) appears to be sufficiently simple.

14. In like manner, if we write, by analogy to the notation of fractional powers of numbers,

$$(c_1, c_2) = (b_1, b_2)^{\frac{\nu}{\mu}}, \qquad (159.)$$

whenever the two couples (b_1, b_2) and (c_1, c_2) are both related as integer powers to one common base couple (a_1, a_2) as follows,

$$(b_1, b_2) = (a_1, a_2)^{\mu}, \quad (c_1, c_2) = (a_1, a_2)^{\nu}, \qquad (160.)$$

(μ and ν being any two whole numbers, of which μ at least is different from 0,) we can easily prove that this *fractional power-couple* (c_1, c_2), or this result of powering the couple (b_1, b_2) by the fractional number $\frac{\nu}{\mu}$, has in general many values, which are all expressed by the formula

$$(c_1, c_2) = (b_1, b_2)^{\frac{\nu}{\mu}} = \text{F}\left(\frac{\nu}{\mu}\,\text{F}^{-1}(b_1, b_2)\right), \qquad (161.)$$

and of which any one may be distinguished from the others by the notation

$$(b_1, b_2)_{\omega}^{\frac{\nu}{\mu}} = \text{F}\left(\frac{\nu}{\mu}\,\text{F}_{\omega}^{-1}(b_1, b_2)\right). \qquad (162.)$$

We may call the couple thus denoted *the ω'th value of the fractional power,* and in particular we may call

$$(b_1, b_2)_{0}^{\frac{\nu}{\mu}} = \text{F}\left(\frac{\nu}{\mu}\,\text{F}_{0}^{-1}(b_1, b_2)\right) \qquad (163.)$$

the *principal value.* The ω'th value may be formed from the principal value, by multiplying it by the ω'th value of the corresponding fractional power of the primary unit, that is, by the following couple,

$$(1, 0)_{\omega}^{\frac{\nu}{\mu}} = \left(\cos \frac{2\,\omega\,\nu\,\pi}{\mu}, \sin \frac{2\,\omega\,\nu\,\pi}{\mu} \right); \qquad (164.)$$

and therefore the number of distinct values of any fractional power of a couple, is equal to the number m of units which remain in the denominator, when the fraction $\frac{\nu}{\mu}$ has been reduced to its simplest possible expression, by the rejection of common factors.

15. Thus, the *powering of any couple* (b_1, b_2) *by any commensurable number* x may be effected by the formula,

$$(b_1, b_2)^x = \text{F}\,(x\,\text{F}^{-1}\,(b_1, b_2)); \qquad (165.)$$

or by these more specific expressions,

$$(b_1, b_2)_{\omega}^x = \text{F}\,(x\,\text{F}_{\omega}^{-1}\,(b_1, b_2))$$
$$= (b_1, b_2)_0^x\,(1, 0)_{\omega}^x, \qquad (166.)$$

in which

$$(1, 0)_{\omega}^x = (\cos \overline{2\,\omega\,x\,\pi}, \sin \overline{2\,\omega\,x\,\pi}): \qquad (167.)$$

and it is natural to extend the same formulæ by definition, for reasons of analogy and continuity, even to the case when the exponent or number x is *incommensurable,* in which latter case *the variety of values of the power is infinite, though no confusion can arise, if each be distinguished from the others by its specific ordinal number,* or *determining integer* ω.

And since the spirit of the present theory leads us to extend all operations with single numbers to operations with number-couples, we shall further define (being authorised by this analogy to do so) that *the powering of any one number-couple* (b_1, b_2) *by any other number-couple* (x_1, x_2) is the calculation of a third number-couple (c_1, c_2), such that

$$(c_1, c_2) = (b_1, b_2)^{(x_1, x_2)} = \text{F}\,((x_1, x_2) \times \text{F}^{-1}\,(b_1, b_2)); \qquad (168.)$$

or more specifically of any one of the infinitely many couples corresponding to the infinite variety of *specific ordinals* or *determining integers* ω, according to this formula,

$$(b_1, b_2)_{\omega}^{(x_1, x_2)} = \text{F}\,((x_1, x_2) \times \text{F}_{\omega}^{-1}\,(b_1, b_2))$$
$$= (b_1, b_2)_0^{(x_1, x_2)}\,(1, 0)_{\omega}^{(x_1, x_2)}, \qquad (169.)$$

in which the factor $(b_1, b_2)_0^{(x_1, x_2)}$ may be called the *principal value* of the general power-couple, and in which the other factor may be calculated by the following expression,

$$(1, 0)_{\omega}^{(x_1, x_2)} = \text{F}((x_1, x_2) \times (0, 2\,\omega\,\pi))$$
$$= \text{F}(-2\,\omega\,\pi\,x_2,\ 2\,\omega\,\pi\,x_1)$$
$$= e_{\omega}^{-2\,\omega\,\pi\,x_2}(\cos 2\,\omega\,\pi\,x_1,\ \sin 2\,\omega\,\pi\,x_1). \quad (170.)$$

For example,

$$(1, 0)_{0}^{(x_1, x_2)} = (1, 0), \quad (171.)$$

and

$$(e, 0)_{0}^{(x_1, x_2)} = \text{F}(x_1, x_2); \quad (172.)$$

also

$$(e, 0)_{\omega}^{(x_1, x_2)} = \text{F}((x_1, x_2) \times (1, 2\,\omega\,\pi)). \quad (173.)$$

On Exponential and Logarithmic Function-Couples in general.

16. It is easy now to discover this general expression for an exponential function-couple:

$$\Phi\,(x_1, x_2) = \text{F}((x_1, x_2) \times (a_1, a_2)); \quad (174.)$$

in which (a_1, a_2) is any constant couple, independent of (x_1, x_2). This *general exponential function* Φ includes the particular function F, and satisfies (as it ought) the condition of the form (128.),

$$\Phi\,(x_1, x_2)\ \Phi\,(y_1, y_2) = \Phi\,(x_1 + y_1, x_2 + y_2); \quad (175.)$$

its *base*, or *base-couple*, which may be denoted for conciseness by (b_1, b_2), is, by the 11th article, the couple

$$(b_1, b_2) = \Phi\,(1, 0) = \text{F}\,(a_1, a_2); \quad (176.)$$

and if we determine that integer number ω which satisfies the conditions

$$a_2 - 2\,\omega\,\pi > -\pi,\quad a_2 - 2\,\omega\,\pi \not> \pi, \quad (177.)$$

we shall have the general transformation

$$\Phi\,(x_1, x_2) = (b_1, b_2)_{\omega}^{(x_1, x_2)}. \quad (178.)$$

And the general *inverse exponential* or *logarithmic function-couple*, which may, by (129.), be thus denoted,

$$(x_1, x_2) = \Phi^{-1}(y_1, y_2), \text{ if } (y_1, y_2) = \Phi(x_1, x_2), \qquad (179.)$$

may also, by (174.) and (176.), be thus expressed:

$$\Phi^{-1}(y_1, y_2) = \frac{\text{F}^{-1}(y_1, y_2)}{\text{F}^{-1}(b_1, b_2)}; \qquad (180.)$$

it involves, therefore, *two arbitrary integer numbers*, when only the couple (y_1, y_2) and the base (b_1, b_2) are given, and it may be thus more fully written,

$$\underset{\omega}{\overset{\omega'}{\Phi}}{}^{-1}(y_1, y_2) = \underset{\omega}{\overset{\omega'}{\log}}{}_{(b_1, b_2)} \cdot (y_1, y_2) = \frac{\underset{\omega'}{\text{F}}{}^{-1}(y_1, y_2)}{\underset{\omega}{\text{F}}{}^{-1}(b_1, b_2)}. \qquad (181.)$$

For example, the general expression for the logarithms of the primary unit (1, 0) to the base (e, 0), is

$$\underset{\omega}{\overset{\omega'}{\log}}{}_{(e, 0)} \cdot (1, 0) = \frac{(0, 2\omega'\pi)}{(1, 2\omega\pi)} = \frac{(2\omega'\pi, 0)}{(2\omega\pi, -1)}, \qquad (182.)$$

or, if we choose to introduce the symbol $\sqrt{-1}$, *as explained in the 13th article*, that is, as denoting the couple (0, 1) according to the law of mixture of numbers with number-couples, then

$$\underset{\omega}{\overset{\omega'}{\log}}{}_{e} \cdot 1 = \frac{2\omega'\pi\sqrt{-1}}{1 + 2\omega\pi\sqrt{-1}} = \frac{2\omega'\pi}{2\omega\pi - \sqrt{-1}}. \qquad (183.)$$

In general,

$$\underset{\omega}{\overset{\omega'}{\log}}{}_{(b_1, b_2)} \cdot (y_1, y_2) = \frac{\underset{0}{\text{F}}{}^{-1}(y_1, y_2) + (0, 2\omega'\pi)}{\underset{0}{\text{F}}{}^{-1}(b_1, b_2) + (0, 2\omega\pi)}. \qquad (184.)$$

The integer number ω may be called the *first specific ordinal*, or simply the ORDER, and the other integer number ω' may be called the *second specific ordinal*, or simply the RANK, of the particular logarithmic function, or *logarithm-couple*, which is determined by these two integer numbers. This existence of *two arbitrary and independent integers in the general expression of a logarithm*, was discovered in the year 1826, by Mr. GRAVES, who published a Memoir upon the subject in the Philosophical Transactions for 1829, and has since made another communication upon the same subject to the British Association for the Advancement of Science, during the meeting of that Association at Edinburgh, in 1834: and it was he who proposed these names of *Orders and Ranks of Logarithms*. But because Mr. GRAVES employed, in his reasoning, the usual principles respecting *Imaginary Quantities*, and was content to prove the symbolical necessity without showing the interpretation, or inner meaning, of his formulæ, the present *Theory of Couples* is published to make manifest that hidden meaning: and to show, by this remarkable instance, that expressions which seem according to common views to be merely symbolical, and quite incapable of being interpreted, may pass into the world of thoughts, and acquire reality and significance, if Algebra be viewed as not a mere Art or Language, but as the Science of Pure Time. The author hopes to publish hereafter many other applications of this view; especially to Equations and Integrals, and to a Theory of Triplets and Sets of Moments, Steps, and Numbers, which includes this Theory of Couples.

THE END.

CPSIA information can be obtained
at www.ICGtesting.com
Printed in the USA
BVHW050243020119
536775BV00027B/1087

9 781173 89830